The Rebellious Duchess

The Rebellious Duchess

The adventures of the
Duchess of Berri and her
attempt to overthrow French monarchy

Paul F. S. Dermoncourt

LEONAUR

The Rebellious Duchess
by Paul F. S. Dermoncourt

First published under the title
Duchess of Berri in La Vendée

Leonaur is an imprint
of Oakpast Ltd

ISBN: 978-1-84677-642-7 (hardcover)
ISBN: 978-1-84677-641-0 (softcover)

http://www.leonaur.com

Contents

DUCHESS OF BERRI

Preface

If I have determined to publish this book, it is neither because I am labouring under an illusion respecting the military importance of the late war in La Vendée, nor because I fancy that I have so particularly distinguished myself in this war, as to induce me to select for publication the present episode of my life in preference to any other.

But if this last campaign in La Vendée be unimportant, in a military sense, it is not so politically. Here, the two principles, for which France divided her sons into two hostile camps, armed against each other ever since 1789, met face to face; and, in this their last duel, the revolutionary principle has killed the monarchical principle, and popular right has reaped the inheritance of divine right.

It is therefore a matte; of great interest, at least such is my view of the case, to contemplate, in its death-throes, a royalty of eight centuries, which, in the days of its youth, produced Philip Augustus and Louis IX., Francis I. and Louis XIV; and in the days of its dotage, Louis XV. and Charles X. It is an extraordinary sight to behold this monarchical body, so gigantic, that at different periods it has covered the whole of Europe by spreading its huge limbs over her, miserably enduring its last agony amid civil war, and breathing out its last sigh in a little corner of France, forsaken by God, and forgotten by the people.

Few persons, I may be allowed to say, are better able than I, to publish such a book as the present, to give the general plan of attack and defence in this war, to pursue it through all its details, both political and military, and, lastly, to enter into those particulars, which impart to a narrative its picturesque character, enduing it with life, and light, and power.

I have stated only that which I believe to be the exact truth. Part of my narrative is founded upon official documents still in my possession; the remainder I obtained from persons upon whose veracity I can depend. Many of the circumstances were related to me by the Duchess of Berri herself.

Paris, September 10th, 1833.

GENERAL DERMONCOURT

The Chateau of La Penissière in La Vendée.

CHAPTER 1

Royal Family in Exile

No sooner had the firing of the 29th of July ceased in the streets of Paris, than the eyes of the French people were directed towards La Vendée. The deposed family were beheld with anxiety taking the road to Cherbourg. A royalist *coup-de-main* might still be attempted, on their passage through Alençon or Vire; or the members of the exiled branch might themselves deceive the vigilance of the commissaries by whom they were accompanied, and take refuge in La Vendée, by crossing the department of the Mayenne, or the Loire-*inférieure*. But nothing of the kind occurred. The proscribed royal family passed through half the kingdom, without its chief making a single attempt to replant the oldest dynasty of Europe in the soil of its growth. A ship was waiting in the port of Cherbourg for these illustrious exiles; and for the third time the wind of revolution wafted them in full sail far away from the shores of France.

La Vendée saw them depart without making a sign of *adieu*: not because she was indifferent to their departure—not because all her blood had flowed forth from the two wounds inflicted upon her by the axe of Robespierre and the sword of Napoleon—nor because her royalist heart, so ardent in civil war, had ceased to beat in Le Bocage; but because, during an earthquake, each first considers his personal safety, and in no province was the shock more violent and unexpected than in La Vendée.

Nevertheless, this calmness, or rather this momentary stupor, did not allay the uneasiness of General Lafayette. La Vendée was the

13

object of his first inquiries after the Revolution of July, and he despatched several agents thither charged with different missions. Alexandre Dumas, among others, was directed to ascertain the possibility of establishing a national guard there.

This idea, which, to those unacquainted with modern La Vendée may have at first appeared impossible to be realized, was, nevertheless, if not a matter of easy, least of very possible execution. La Vendée, in 1830, was no longer the same as in 1794: its population, formerly divided into nobles and farmers only, had since the latter period produced a class which had glided in between the two others—namely, the owners of national property. Although the sale of national property, a great territorial measure originating with the convention, was with difficulty effected in this province, then distracted by civil war, there are, nevertheless, few great landowners in it who have not left some shreds of their inheritance in the hands of the revolution.

These shreds have constituted a secondary property, in which the spirit of improvement and of liberty exists; because improvement and liberty can alone secure the peaceable possession of it, and all counter-revolution must naturally throw a doubt upon the legality of the tenure by which it is held. It is this class of property which, by its reaction upon the nobility, who are superior in fortune to those holding it, the latter being however superior in number, has sent to the legislature, ever since 1815, patriot deputies, whose presence there might seem a problem without this explanation.

The owners of this property, were delighted at the revolution of 1830, because they saw that it was a child of that of 1793; they would therefore naturally consider it a consecration of the sale of national property, and consequently support it with all their might. And what better means could they find of supporting it, than by the establishment of a national guard to maintain the peace of the province, and which, being composed of a class sufficiently numerous to form a majority at the elections, was also sufficiently numerous to awe its enemies into peace? General Lafayette's plan was therefore perfectly logical in its conception, and very possible of execution.

A residence of two months in the departments of Loire-inférieure, Morbihan, and Maine-et-Loire, convinced Alexandre Dumas that it was not only an excellent measure to adopt, but likewise that its execution was urgent. He had seen scattered on all sides, those seeds of civil war which germinate so powerfully in the soil of La Vendée. He had passed through royalist crowds publicly assembled at the Chateaux of Combouros, Herbiers, and Boissière du Doré. He had designated by name the modern Bonchamps and D'Elbées, who were to take a part in the new civil war; and, aided by the counsels of men inhabiting the country, he had pointed out the means of preventing such war. Unfortunately, on his return to Paris, a reaction had already taken place in the government; General Lafayette had preserved a mere nominal influence in the new administration, and could therefore only refer his agent to M. Guizot, Minister of the Interior.

This statesman listened to the information afforded him, with that self-sufficiency which everyone knows him to possess; and replied, that he also had felt the pulse of La Vendée, and, having found it rather agitated, had despatched an excellent physician to its relief, in the person of M. de Saint-Aignan, Prefect of Nantes.

Under any other circumstances, or in any other province, the choice of M. de Saint-Aignan would have been a proof of sagacity on the part of the government; M. de Saint-Aignan being both an honest man and an able administrator. But he was the last man who ought to have been appointed prefect of Nantes, because he is connected, through his family, with the entire Vendean aristocracy. Thus, he had scarcely reached that city, before he so strongly felt the delicacy of his situation, that he tendered his resignation, which was refused. M. de Saint-Aignan was therefore placed between his affections and his duty; nevertheless, such was his probity, that not a single individual at Nantes ever doubted that on all occasions he made his affections yield to his duty.

It was not however less an error in the Government to have appointed him; for at the very outset he excited mistrust, over which his long and at last well-known integrity could alone triumph. It is true that at the period when everyone did him justice, he was brutally dismissed, and M. Maurice Duval appointed in his stead. The extraordinary reception of the latter gentleman at Nantes, which we shall relate in its proper place, shows that there was a unanimity of feeling towards him as powerful, if not so flattering, as that entertained towards M. de Saint-Aignan.

Alexandre Dumas, not discouraged by the minister's reception, carried his report to the king, who after reading it, told him that he had looked upon such matters with the eye of a poet.

"Sir," he replied, "the Latins termed poets *Vates.*" On saying this he withdrew.

On his return to his own house, he found a letter from General Lamarque, military commandant of La Vendée, requesting to see him on the same day, this general having been made acquainted with his return by General Lafayette.

In the evening he waited on General Lamarque, who next day set out for Nantes, but whose dismissal followed him some hours after, and reached him at Angers.

This dismissal was the result of one of those contemptible combinations which ministers pompously decorate with the term of "high political views;" and I think the following explanation will show that my assertion in this respect is well founded. Our revolution, which had been so instantaneous, and which we had, at first, considered so complete, had made its cry of freedom resound through Belgium, and Italy, and Poland. These nations had called out loudly, "France, help us!" and such an appeal is always heard by the French nation.

The most lively popular sympathy had consequently burst forth in our cities and our provinces, in favour of those revolutions which resembled ours, being partial eruptions at a distance from the great volcano, whose centre was at Paris. Shouts of "Italy, Belgium, Poland, forever!" filled our streets, and entered through every door and window, even into the royal palace, and into the palaces of the king's ministers. At this period the great voice of the people was still listened to, and they who governed were forced to promise, upon their honour, that the nationality of Belgium, and Italy, and Poland, should not perish.

At length the shouts of joy uttered by foreign patriots became cries of distress; it was time to save Belgium by uniting it to France, Italy by sending to its aid one of those old generals[1] who would have shown the way thither to a new army, and Poland, by effecting a diversion to the Czar's projects, and promoting, which was then very easy, a rising in Turkey on the one hand, and in Persia on the other.[2]

We then should have left Russia, thus placed within a triangle of enemies, to get out of the scrape in the best manner she could, and have carried to the other two nations, our neighbours, the more efficacious aid of our presence and our armies. The people, always certain and powerful in instinct, so strongly felt the possibility of effecting these three results, though they could not explain the means whereby, that they hailed with cries of applause the proclamation of the ministerial system of non-intervention, and the king's promise that the nationality of Poland should not be suffered to perish.

The king and his ministers fully understood their situation: they must either declare war or become perjured;—in the former case, they should come to a rupture with kings, in the latter, with the people. One sole alternative remained: this was to prove to the country that the French nation was too much occupied with its own concerns to be able to attend to those of other nations. This was like giving a man an inflammation of the bowels in order that, being absorbed by his own pain, he should be unable to sympathize in the pains of others. A trifling civil war in La Vendée would marvellously second such views. It accordingly became expedient to withdraw from that province, upon which such an experiment was to be tried, every man of firmness capable of putting down insurrection at its very commencement, and every man of talent who might have been able to detect the real object

1. Marshal Allison, ambassador at Vienna, so strongly felt the necessity of such a measure, that he proposed to the government to place twenty thousand men in observation upon the frontier of Piedmont. This military demonstration would, in his opinion, alone prove sufficient to neutralize the influence of Austria.
2. It is to this advice, which he was imprudent enough to give, that General Guilleminot was indebted for his recall from the embassy to Constantinople.

of such insurrection. Now General Lamarque, being gifted with both talents and firmness, time was not even allowed him, as we have before shown, to reach the place of his command.

He was succeeded by General Bonnet; and in the latter appointment the government also made a sad mistake. Bonnet is a man formed upon the same military model as Lamarque;—full of honour and experience—calm, resolute, capable of combining energy with moderation, a good administrator, and a man of first-rate military talent. He had scarcely reached Nantes, before he perceived in the surrounding departments revolt in progress of ostensible organization, and, by means of its agents in that city, converging thither as to a nucleus. General Bonnet considered it his duty, before he took any vigorous measures, to apply for instructions to the government. Ministers were not of his opinion, and directed him to temporise. General Bonnet therefore sent in his resignation.

General Solignac took his place; and from that period, the affairs of La Vendée proceeded according to the will of the ministers.

Meanwhile, the government pursued a line of foreign policy in keeping with that adopted at home. Louis-Philippe refused a king to Belgium, but gave it a queen; and we purchased the alliance of Great Britain by leaving to that power a hunting-box on the Continent, as at the period when William the Conqueror possessed Normandy. We had, moreover, sent a garrison to Ancona; but to make the Holy Father forget the somewhat rude manner in which the troops composing it had knocked at the gates of the town, our soldiers received orders to look calmly on, with ported arms, at the hanging of the Romagnese patriots.

We had allowed the capital of Poland to be taken, but our fears concerning the fate of the Poles were removed by the information that the most perfect order reigned at Warsaw. The Polish martyrs might therefore sleep undisturbed in their tombs. Thanks to this policy, there was no longer any doubt with regard to the peaceable determinations, if not to the pacific feelings of the Holy Alliance towards France. This was all we wanted; our honour was satisfied by it, after the manner, it is true, in which a man whose nose has been pulled calls out his aggressor, and then makes him an apology upon the ground.

These promises of external peace, made under the concessions of our ministers, however they may have caused the nation to blush, did not the less attain the desired end. A counter-revolutionary reaction had taken place, not only in the government but in public feeling; riots in the metropolis had indeed served as a protest against it, but ministers had *resigned* themselves to having the riots put down with grape-shot. The civil war in La Vendée became therefore a useless superfluity, and the government thought that it was high time to bring it to a conclusion.

CHAPTER 2

Departure to Nantes

It was at this period that I was appointed to the command of the military sub-division at Nantes.

At my time of life, when a man may speak of himself with the same freedom he would use in speaking of another, I may be allowed to say, that my appointment was a proof that ministers would no longer trifle with the insurgents of La Vendée. Forty-four years' service in Europe, in Asia, in America, and in Africa—the giant battles in which I have shared, and compared with which our battles of the present day are mere skirmishes, have made me careless of life, and the sword fit lightly to my hand. Moreover, my disgrace under the restoration, during the existence of which I would not re-enter the service—the active part I took in the conspiracy of Belfort, in which I was near losing my head—and the promptitude with which I offered my services to the provisional government of July 1830, constituted a sure moral pledge to the government of the zeal with which I would smite the Chouans. I accordingly took my departure for Nantes.

I was now about to see my old friends the Vendeans once more; but this time we were not to part without saying to each other some of those sharp words which tend to pierce a man's body through and through. The country was not wholly unknown to me; the manner of fighting with its inhabitants was familiar to me, and the campaigns I had served in Spain, had kept me in good practice of this warfare of hedges and ravines; a stupid and bad kind of warfare, it is true, but which it was necessary to accept for want of a better.

So much has been said of La Vendée within the last forty years, that no one is ignorant of the topographic peculiarities which render its mode of waging war distinct from every other. The ordinary theories of strategy are quite inapplicable to this French Catalonia: war is here a game played with the sword, by inspiration and by caprice, and the success of which, in the two first means, depends upon physical courage, and in the last, upon chance.

Nevertheless, I was far from imagining, and the result has shown that I was right, that this war would ever become so desperate, and so determined, as that of 1794. I have already explained how a new class of inhabitants, by gliding among the great landowners, had introduced a point of opposition among the population; and I will now show how a different cause had produced an effect absolutely similar among the peasantry.

The eternal wars of Napoleon had, as we all know, neces-sitated conscriptional levies, which, during the latter part of his reign, had become more and more frequent. The five depart-ments which the Chouans unite under the generic name of La Vendée, had, like every other department, been subjected to this species of decimation; and, among the individuals thus forced to follow the conqueror in his armed promenades, were many of the children of La Vendée. Such among the latter as did not remain scattered over the field of battle, returned home with ideas very differ-ent from those with which they had set out.

Their notions had been changed by the new world they had lived in, and still more by their contact with men to whom hatred of the Bourbons seemed a paramount duty. To these, the fall of Napoleon was a source of grief—the entrance of the allied troops, a disgrace; and from this period they had maintained patriotic opinions, more deeply implanted in their bosoms by the constant sight of their crosses and their epaulets suspended over their mantel-pieces, than the feelings of their adversaries were nurtured by the sight of the bleeding heart and English carbine.

Trade had likewise operated its work of improvement, being

carried on by means of the new roads cut by Napoleon through beds of solid rock. And, in fact, on both sides bordering upon the highways, the most patriotic spirit everywhere reigns; but this feeling cools in proportion as you advance on either side into the less frequented parts of the country, and in a short time totally disappears. Thanks to these new elements, which have operated in favour of our modern ideas, the seeds of civil war have become less difficult to root out in La Vendée.

The part of the country in which my new command lay, was more particularly the one upon whose inhabitants I most depended for support against rebellion. A great city formed its centre, and trade and industry threw forth diverging *radii* upon a circle of three or four leagues around it. The department of the Loire-inférieure is formed of a portion of Upper Britanny, the old country of Mauge, that of Retz, and the Upper and Lower Marches. It touches the department of Mayenne on the north-east, extends towards the west by a curve line which separates it from the departments of Ile-et-Vilaine, and Morbihan, and reaches the sea on that side.

On the south it runs like the head of a lance into La Vendée, whilst on the east it is divided from the. department of Maine-et-Loire, and from La Vendée, by a line of separation, in the centre of which stands the pretty little town of Clisson serving as its advanced sentinel. It is divided into five districts, and forty-five cantons; its surface contains three hundred and thirty-six square leagues; it comprises two hundred and seven communes, and has three hundred and fifty thousand inhabitants. Its extreme breadth from north to south is about twenty-three ordinary leagues, and its length from east to west about twenty-five. The Loire, entering its territory at Ingrande, runs through its length, and discharges itself into the sea within sight of St. Nazaire and Paimboeuf.

Nantes, its capital, is situated at the conflux of three rivers, upon an acclivity extending from east to west. To the south runs the Loire, to which the Erdre adds its waters after washing the northern flanks of the city. On the opposite side of its bridges and facing its quay, the Sévre-Nantaise, which runs from Parthenay, also falls into the Loire. The verdant hills which surround the city, are interspersed with picturesque country-houses, with white walls, and from the windows of which the movement of a population of eighty thousand inhabitants may be seen active and busy, in the three hundred streets of the city, in its thirty squares, and from one end to the other of its eighteen bridges.

In a military point of view, Nantes has no other means of defence than the arms and courage of its inhabitants. It is open on all sides; rich and confident, as if civil war had never threatened to disturb its tranquillity. And yet its strategical situation forms a most important point, as by means of its bridges, it unites the opposite banks of the Loire, and naturally becomes the pivot of all operations undertaken in La Vendée on the one side, and in Britanny on the other.

Thus, in three successive wars, it has formed the point constantly aimed at by the Vendean generals. Its castle alone, built in the thirteenth century, and flanked with towers, is secure from a *coup-de-main*, though not from a regular siege.

There are, as I have already stated, but few high roads throughout the country, and these are almost all modern. There are four on the right bank of the Loire, and only two on the left.

The first, on the right bank, leads to Paris through Ancenis and Ange.

The second, to Alençon and Caën, through Chateaubriand.

The third, to Rennes, through Nozai and Derval.

The fourth to Brest, through Savenai.

Those on the left bank lead:

The first from Nantes to Rochelle through Montaigu.

The second from Nantes to Paimboeuf.

Besides these great highways, there exist secondary and cross-roads. Upon the right bank are one from Ancenis to Redon, through Nort and Blain; one to the same place, from Chateaubriand, through Derval; a third from Chateaubriand to Angers, through Candé; and a fourth from St. Nizaire to Roch-Berraud, through Guerande. On the left bank, the cross-roads lead from Nantes: 1st, to Beaupréau, through Vallet; 2nd, to Mortagne and

Cholet, through Clisson; 3rd, to the Sables-d'Olonne through Legé; 4th, to Challans by Machecoul.

But these roads are scarcely more favourable to military operations than the smaller cross-roads. Bordered on either side with wide and deep ditches, bushes, and trees, sometimes between two slopes, they give the Chouans great facility in forming ambuscades on their whole length. Besides this, each individual estate, great and small, is surrounded with a hedge; and these estates communicate with one another, only by means of small wickets made of the same materials as the enclosure.

The inhabitants of the country alone can discover these openings, termed *échaliers;* and if pursued, can raise a wicket and replace it so as to render the spot where they passed imperceptible to their pursuers. Thus, a Vendean, as I have already stated, foils every strategic calculation of the military art, especially when made for open plains.

As for the army which you expect every instant to encounter, it vanishes like smoke, for in truth it has no existence.

When a day is fixed on to strike a blow, at daybreak or even during the night, the tocsin is sounded in the village designated as the point of union. The neighbouring villages reply in the same manner, and the villagers quit their cottages, if it be in the night, or their ploughs if in the day, throwing upon their shoulder the gun which they scarcely ever quit.

Having stuffed their belt with cartridges, they tie their handkerchief round a broad-brimmed hat which shades their sun-burnt countenance; stop at their church to utter a short prayer; then, inspired with a two-fold faith, in God and in the justice of their cause, they wend their way from all parts of the country to the common centre.

Their chiefs soon arrive, who acquaint them with the cause of their being assembled; and if the object be to attack some patriot column, these chiefs state the road which the column will pursue, and the hour it will pass. Then, when this information is well understood by all, the chief in command gives them the plan of the battle in the following words:

"Eparpillez vous, mes gars!"
"Scatter yourselves my fine fellows!"

Immediately each breaks, not from the ranks, but from the group, marches off his own way, proceeds onward with precaution and in silence, and in a short time every tree, every bush, every tuft of furze bordering either side of the high road, conceals a peasant with a gun in one hand and supporting himself with the other, crouched like a wild beast, without motion and scarcely breathing.

Meanwhile, the patriot column, uneasy at the thought of some unknown danger, advances towards the defile, preceded by scouts who pass without seeing, touch without feeling, and are allowed to go by scathless. But the moment the detachment is in the middle of the pass, jammed in between two sloping banks, as if it were in an immense rut, and unable to deploy either to the right or to the left,—a cry, sometimes an imitation of that of an owl, issues from one extremity, and is repeated along the whole line of ambuscade.

This indicates that each is at his post. A human cry succeeds, one of war and of death. In an instant each bush, each tuft of furze, glares with a sudden flash, and a shower of balls strike whole files of soldiers to the earth, without their being able to perceive the enemies who slaughter them.

The dead and wounded lie piled upon each other on the road; and if the column is not thrown into disorder, and the voices of the officers are heard above the firing—if, in short, the troops attempt to grapple body to body with their assailants, who strike without showing themselves—if they climb the slope like a glacis, and scale the hedge like a wall, the peasants have already had time to retire behind a second inclosure, whence the invisible firing recommences as murderous as before.

Should this second hedge be stormed in the same manner, ten, twenty, nay, a hundred similar intrenchments offer successive shelters to this destructive retreat: for the country is thus divided for the security of the children of the soil, which seems to show a maternal solicitude for their preservation, by offering them a shelter everywhere, and their enemies everywhere a grave.

What we have just stated explains how the convention, which

had conquered fourteen armies commanded by kings and princes, could never pacify La Vendée, kept in a state of rebellion by a few peasants; and how Napoleon, who dictated his will to the whole of Europe, could never succeed in getting his orders executed in three of the departments of France.

CHAPTER 3

Arrival in Nantes

I arrived at Nantes on the 1st of May; and, after calling upon General Solignac, my commanding officer, and upon the civil authorities, I set out to visit the cantonments under my command.

These were divided into five military districts: three upon the right and two upon the left bank. The districts on the right bank were, Chateaubriand, Ancenis, and Savenai; those on the left bank were, Machecoul and Clisson.

Each of these districts, commanded by a *chef-de-bataillon*, was the centre of several secondary cantonments, variable at my will and according to the wants of the service. These secondary cantonments were under the command of captains; and beyond them, still smaller detachments, commanded by lieutenants or sub-lieutenants, advanced like sentinels into the suspected country.

These cantonments formed, round Nantes, a moving belt of about three thousand five hundred men.[1] By this arrangement, the regiments were made to acquire an exact knowledge of the country, as likely to be very useful to them on the day of a battle. The thirty-second regiment of the line in particular, which has been so stationed ever since the beginning of 1831, is at present as well acquainted with the worst passes of La Vendée as the most able of the Chouans. Besides this, it is excellent policy to station regiments in the same villages during several months in succession, as it leads to an intimacy between the soldiers and the inhabitants, and the

---

1. When I arrived in the department, I had only at my disposal the 32nd regiment of the line, and a battalion of the 39th cantoned in the district of Clisson.

former thereby become acquainted with all the movements of the Chouans.

In my first inspection of these districts, I perceived, by the movements of the peasantry, and by the communications which I detected between Nantes and La Vendée, that an extensive insurrection was hatching, and would soon burst forth. The nobles were training the peasants to military exercises in their barns, and the popish priests not only did not sing, during the church service, the *"Domine salvum fac regem Philippura,"*[2] but from the pulpit recommended Henry V. King of France, and Marie-Caroline, Regent, to the prayers of the faithful.

The very air from La Vendée was impregnated with a smell of war, which we old soldiers know by instinct, no matter from what quarter it comes; and each puff of wind brought even into our guard-houses proclamations like the following:

Inhabitants of the Country,

The son of the regicide, he whose bloody standard appeared like a sign of desolation in your fields, has at length thrown off the mask. He has just confessed his hatred of that holy religion which your fathers transmitted to you at the expense of their best blood. He had already permitted brigands to pull down churches, drag the sacred vessels through the streets of Paris, and commit all sorts of abominations. This was, to him, only a first step in the career of sacrilege: learn now what he has done; ending as Bonaparte ended, he has dared to attack even the pope himself. Soldiers who are the blind instruments of his impiety, have entered, as enemies, a city under the domination of the Holy See; they surprised it by night, and the venerable chief of our religion has in vain protested against this horrible crime. Oh! do not doubt it—an avenging God is pursuing Louis-Philippe! This last crime has filled the measure of his iniquity, and the day of deliverance is approaching.

France, so unhappy ever since the resumption of the revolu-

---

2. See Appendix No. 1.

tionary colours, will soon see its saviour appear.
Printing-office of Henry V.

Who this saviour was—what chief was to become the leader of the civil war, and head the insurrection, was still unknown to us. Our doubts, however, upon this point, were soon set at rest.

By a telegraphic dispatch, we were made acquainted with the appearance of the Duchess of Berri, within sight of the French coast; and the very next day, the *Moniteur* gave us an account of the riots at Marseilles. As these riots had been suppressed, and the Duchess not taken, it was evident that we should soon have her in La Vendée. I consequently gave directions to maintain the greatest vigilance upon the whole of our military line, convinced as I was that we should soon obtain positive intelligence,[3] concerning her motions.

On the 24th of May I received, during the absence of General Solignac, the following report brought to me by an orderly of *gendarmerie*. It was addressed to my commanding officer by General Mocquery, commandant of the department of La Vendée, and was the flash of the priming generally seen before the report of the gun is heard.

Head-quarters, Bressuire, May 24th, 1832.
 General,
A band of Carlists, about a hundred strong, commanded by Diot and Robert, was met yesterday at Amailloux and dispersed by a moveable detachment. A certain M. Desménard, whose passport was delivered to him at Saintes, and M. de Chierre, a *chef-d'escadron* of the staff, formerly *aid-de-camp* to General Lauriston, and bearing a *port-d'armes* delivered at Niort, have been I 'ought to me at Bressuire, as forming part of this band of rebels. I have delivered them over to the *Procureur du Roi,* who has committed them to the common jail. M. de Chierre announces for this day (24th) a movement of the legitimatists on every point of La Vendée and of the south.

---

3. See Appendix, Nos. 2, 3, and 4.

In haste, I have despatched orders for movements, and for re-doubled vigilance on every point under my command. I will regularly report to you everything that takes place. I have the honour, &c.

B. Mocquery,
Marechal de Camp.

P.S. M. de Chierre was coming from Exeuil (Deux Sevres), and had about him nine hundred *francs*, which the *chef-de-bataillon* Chardron has been desirous of preserving to be returned to the person to whom it belongs. M. Desménard had only thirty-five *francs*.

I immediately despatched a copy of this report to the war minister, together with an account of the measures I had adopted to put down the movement of which M. de Chierre had given information, and which circumstances, then unknown to us, had caused to be adjourned.

Next day (23rd) there came a fresh *estafette*, with another report from an officer of the 32nd, commanding the cantonment of Guen-rouet, addressed to his *chef-de-bataillon* who commanded the district of Chateaubriand. All doubt was now removed: the Duchess of Berri had crossed the kingdom, and was in La Vendée. This report is the first official document announcing her presence. I give it pre-cisely as it reached us; were I to alter its style its peculiar character would be destroyed.

"Guenrouet, May 25th, 1832.

"Commandant,

"Yesterday, in the course of the day, M. de Coislin (Adol-phe) the eldest son, sent to me to ask for an interview at eleven o'clock at night, in a wood a quarter of a league from Guenrouet, in order to converse about my own interests and those of the country. At eleven o'clock I was at the place appointed, which M. de Coislin reached a short time after. The following is, as nearly as possible, a summary of our con-ference, which lasted till midnight.

"I began by stating to M. de Coislin that if the things he had to confide to me were of a nature to oblige me to preserve secrecy, or to endanger in the slightest degree the safety of the country, I begged he would keep them to himself.

"'Sir,' he replied; 'what I have to tell you is known to everybody, or at all events will soon be so. The Duchess of Berri is in this country, I give you my word of honour; I have not seen her, but my father has seen and spoken to her. The riots which took place at Marseilles were got up only to draw the attention of Government to that point, whilst the duchess landed on another part of the coast, and crossed the whole of France in order to reach La Vendée, where she now is.'

"'Well, Sir,' I said, 'we shall capture her, if she is in La Vendée.'

"'Sir, we will make a rampart of our bodies to protect her.'

"'Sir, we will throw it down.'

"'Sir, the duchess has called to her standard all the persons who are devoted to her. She does not yet appear; but she will do so shortly, and restore to her country the happiness it has lost since the revolution. During the struggle in July 1830, my father and I had assembled some forces to march to the assistance of General Despinois; but the king would not accept our services, and we returned to our homes. For three months we remained quiet, in the hope that Louis-Philippe might perhaps render France happy; but when we saw the turn which things took, we worked without intermission to reach the point we have now attained. Let us calmly reflect, Sir; civil war is a very cruel thing, and it is unfortunate to be obliged to have recourse to it; but it will soon break out. We will not begin it; we will never begin to fire on the troops. They will challenge us with—"Who goes there?" we will answer "Friends;" we will offer them our hands, and will invite them to join our ranks. Your military situation is a very delicate one, Sir: you have on the one hand subordination and orders, and on the other your duty as a Frenchman. Will you fire at your countrymen? The Duchess of Berri only, and her son, Henry V. can extricate France from the unhappy situation in which it is placed. We ought, therefore, all to co-operate towards the same end, by calling them among us, and thus contribute to the happiness of our country.'

"After having listened, not without impatience, to such a discourse, I replied to the following effect.

"'You place the happiness of France, Sir, in a very different point of view from the one I have taken. It is useless to discuss this point. I am a French officer, and my opinion, like that of every officer in the army, is, that whoever devotes himself to the service of his country is bound to shed every drop of his blood in its defence. Rise, and attack us; if on our challenge you reply 'Friends!' we will tell you that we do not acknowledge any friends bearing the white flag; if you do not then retire, we will fire at you, because whoever takes up arms against his country ought to be considered an enemy. Under such circumstances you are no longer our countrymen.

"'The more delicate my military situation, the greater honour do I take to myself for conscientiously fulfilling all the obligations it imposes. Moreover, Sir, subordination and my duty as a Frenchman go hand in hand. My commanding officers will never give me any orders that can prevent me from fulfilling my duties as a French citizen.

"'I do not believe in the presence of the Duchess of Berri in La Vendée; and even if she were there, it would tend only to hasten the signal of a war which you may rely upon it, Sir, will turn out entirely to the disadvantage of your cause. I know not whether, by urging me to meet you here, it was your intention to seduce me to join your party. I would gladly suppose, Sir, that, having been a soldier, such a thing would be too repugnant to your feelings. If, however, the contrary were the case, I should much pity the party obliged to support itself by such means. I wish you a good night. When we meet again, Sir, I trust we shall not be armed against each other.'

"'So do I,' he replied, 'but I fear it not.'"

On the same day a copy of this report was forwarded to Paris, and the *Moniteur* of the 2nd of June informed the whole of France that the Duchess of Berri was already in La Vendée, whilst the police were still in search of her in the south of France.

CHAPTER 4

Return to France

This is, I imagine, the right place for giving some particulars which I have since obtained, concerning the motives that induced the Duchess of Berri to return to France, her landing on the coast near Marseilles, and her unobstructed journey through the south and west of France.

Charles X., after his exile from France, and notwithstanding his abdication and that of his son, would never consent to give the title of Regent to the Duchess of Berri, lest he should thereby be deprived of the direction of the education of the Duke of Bordeaux.

The Duchess of Berri, however, after she had formed the resolution of quitting her family and entering France, but before she had fixed upon the time for doing so, obtained from the ex-king, a letter dated from Edinburgh and addressed to the royalists of France, the object of which was to induce these latter to acknowledge Marie Caroline, Duchess of Berri, as Regent of that kingdom.

Having got this letter, the duchess left England with a few courtiers who had remained faithful to her. On the 17th of June 1831, she passed through Holland. Having remained a day or two at Frankfort, and the same period at Mayence, she crossed Switzerland, entered Piedmont, and, under the name of the Countess Sagana, at length stopped at Sestri, a small town situated twelve leagues from Genoa, and forming part of the dominions of King Charles Albert.

Her *incognito* was, however, quite useless, because it did not extend to the individuals by whom she was accompanied. She might be traced from inn to inn; for in every innkeeper's book were to be seen the signatures of M. de Ménars, M. de Duras, and others of her suite.

The royalists of France, who had been informed of the Duchess of Berri's approach towards the French frontier, covered the roads of Lombardy and Piedmont; and everybody knew her under the name of the Countess de Sagana. She herself took no trouble to conceal her real name. Every Sunday she went to a church situated about two hundred yards from her place of residence, on foot, and generally through a lane of individuals attracted by the curiosity of seeing her followed by the same suite that attended her at Paris, and her head covered with nothing but a piece of lace, termed by the Genoese ladies *mesaro*, and which they put on with such graceful coquetry.

The French Government was, therefore, soon made acquainted with the presence of the Duchess of Berri in Piedmont, and took offence accordingly. M. de Cases, the French consul at Genoa, knew that the hotels of that city were crowded with Frenchmen, none of whom came to him to have their passports countersigned. The fact is, most of the royalists had obtained passports from foreign embassies, and having for a time become British, German, or Italian subjects, presented their passports, under assumed names, at the embassies of their adopted nations.

Thus, at the hotel of Malta, at Genoa, there were a dozen travellers of all nations in Europe, except France, who, when assembled together, spoke nothing but French, and with as pure an accent as M. de Cases himself. This gave the consul great annoyance, and he referred the matter to his government. A letter from the cabinet of the Tuileries was immediately addressed to the Sardinian government, complaining that Charles Albert was nurturing a conspiracy in his dominions, which could be directed only against France.

Charles Albert then wrote a letter to the Duchess of Berri, entering into the particulars of the political system adopted by foreign states with regard to France. He informed her that the sovereigns of Europe, too much harassed themselves by the popular discontent manifested in their own dominions, to meddle with other countries, so long as it could be avoided, were unwilling to wage a war of principles with France, as they should be but badly seconded by their own subjects. It was their intention, however, to unite against the French nation on the slightest aggression which could afford them a plausible pretence for doing so.

This long diplomatic letter concluded by a polite request, the motives for which were stated at length, but which was not less a peremptory order, that the duchess would quit the Sardinian states, her residence in them having become too notorious. But she might return thither whenever she thought proper to do so, under a stricter *incognito*, so that the King of Sardinia might be able to deny to Louis-Philippe that she was in his dominions.

This letter exasperated the duchess, whose independent and despotic character would lead her to undergo any kind of danger and fatigue rather than support the slightest contradiction to her will She could not comprehend how Charles Albert, whom she had seen with epaulets of red wool, join, as a volunteer, the French army destined to conquer Spain, could so soon forget the kind reception he had met with at the court of Charles X.; and how, eight years after, having himself become a king, he could order her to quit his dominions. This letter was a source of humiliation to which she constantly alluded in her conversation with those Frenchmen who went to Sestri to receive her commands.

"Royalty is disappearing," she said to one of them, "like architecture. My great-grandfather built palaces, my grandfather built houses, my father built huts, and my brother will no doubt build rats' nests. But God willing, my son, when it comes to his turn, shall build palaces again."

At length the duchess made up her mind to leave Piedmont, pledging herself to the royalists, whose visits she had received at Sestri, to enter France at their very first call, and whenever they thought a favourable opportunity offered. After staying a few days at Modena, she went through Tuscany, and proceeded to Rome. It was at this period that the Pope presented Deutz to her.

Meanwhile, the individuals who surrounded the Duchess of Berri, every one of whom held by anticipation very important appointments under the regent Marie Caroline, hastened, with all their powers of persuasion, her landing upon the coast of France. To effect this purpose, a sort of league was formed among these individuals, to conceal from the duchess all news which did not exactly tally with their views. The accounts from France which represented the success of an insurrection as a thing impossible, even for. an instant, were carefully kept from her, or else softened down, whilst everything that could encourage her to make the attempt was greatly exaggerated.

Nevertheless, every prudent man, however warmly he might be attached to the restoration of her son, wrote to her not to come. The western provinces could not assume any influence over the destinies of France, unless supported either by a rising in the south or by a foreign invasion. In the former case, these provinces would, through Bordeaux, become connected with Marseilles, and Toulouse, and thus one half of France would declare for Henry V.; in the latter, the duchess, who had constantly evinced a strong repugnance to a restoration like those of 1814 and 1815, would throw herself, with her son, into La Vendée, protest against foreign armies entering France, rally the nation around her, and march at its head against the common enemy. Of these two plans, one was almost sure, the other almost national.

Unfortunately for Her Royal Highness, the private interests of those by whom she was surrounded obscured the political atmosphere through which she beheld France. The chance of foreign invasion was lost, from the very moment when the French Government, yielding to the policy imposed by foreign cabinets, had allowed the Italian patriots to be hanged, and those of Poland to be butchered.

It was the least thing that the grateful foreign potentates could do, after concessions so little in harmony with the system of non-intervention, and after the royal speech, to allow Louis-Philippe quietly to retain his rank among the crowned members of the Holy Alliance. The chance of an insurrection in the south was therefore the only one that remained.

The consequence of all this was that the duchess's little court used all their eloquence in persuading her that the whole of France was ready to rise in her favour. The discontent in the south was described to her as a flagrant insurrection, the fidelity of La Vendée as an organized rising, and the republican movement as a royalist revolt. She was therefore completely deceived with regard to public feeling in France; and this, together with her own adventurous and restless character, contributed, with the personal interests of her courtiers, to hasten the moment of her enterprise, which she has herself since termed a foolish attempt.

Moreover, some recently received letters from France contained such promises of fidelity to her, that they added considerably to her illusion. We have these letters before us, and the blindness or imprudence of those who wrote them seems to us almost incredible.

It is true, that these same individuals deserted the duchess the moment they found that there was any danger in remaining with her. One of them, a peer of France, a man who well knew the country, and whose opinion at such a juncture was peremptory, wrote to her to beg she would hasten the moment of our deliverance!

Let your Royal Highness but come to La Vendée, and you shall see that my belly, though of European fame from its size, will not prevent me from leaping both hedges and ditches.

General Dermoncourt, no doubt to spare the feelings of an individual whom he may sometimes meet in society, has omitted the name of the very delicate author of this letter; but as we have no scruples of the same kind, and the letter itself is in the hands of the French Government, we here state that the writer is M. Humbert de Sesmaisons, Peer of France, a gentleman as remarkable for the emptiness of his head as for the enormity of his paunch—the largest in France, perhaps in all Europe.

He is truly an *"Epicuri de grege porcus;"* swinish in his manner of feeding, in his habits, and, as our fair readers may perceive by his letter, in his mode of writing, even to a lady of the highest rank and lineage. Nevertheless he is a staunch aristocrat and a most obsequious courtier, though his notions of courtly bearing are not such as would find favour among the noble dames who grace the court of William IV.

A ludicrous anecdote is related of this gentleman.

Whenever he travels by the diligence—for peers of France sometimes use such a conveyance—betakes two places, in order that he may find plenty of room for his rotundity. On one of these occasions, having sent his servant to bespeak the usual number of places, the poor man took one in the interior and the other in the *coupe*. It seems that these were the only two left. Now, as M. de Sesmaison could not divide himself into two parts, the vehicle started without him. The consequence was that his journey was deferred, and the luckless author of the mistake discharged.—Tr.

Another from the Marquis de Coislin arrived in December 1831. We are ignorant of its contents but the answer of the duchess [1] enables us to guess them.

I have long known, my dear de Coislin, the zeal and devotion of you and yours to my son's cause; and it is a pleasure to me to repeat to you, that on many future occasions I shall depend entirely upon you, as you may also depend upon my gratitude.
Marie Caroline.
December 14th, 1831.

Such counsels were, it must be admitted, well calculated to mislead a woman whose character naturally urged her to dangerous undertakings. It was therefore decided, that public feeling towards her in France had reached the necessary degree of maturity; and all was accordingly prepared for the great undertaking so impatiently looked for by the supporters of legitimacy. The royalists of France, more especially those in the south and the west, were therefore warned to hold themselves in readiness.

The letter forwarded to them was written in sympathetic ink. We give it, with its translation; the phrase by which it was deciphered is

---

1. Seized at the *Chateau* of La Chaslière

the following:—"*Lorsqu'il est du droit commun.*" (When it appertains to the comman law.) It contains twenty-four letters, substituted for the twenty-four letters of the alphabet.

```
        |  |    |  |||||  |  | |
• Lorsqu'il est du droit commun.
Abcdefgh ijk lm nopqr stu v x y.
```

```
                        |  | |        | |      |
  " Je ferai savoir à  dldoqc  l  ldiqtc  qo  l
|  | |    |      | |      |        |  | |
tqddqc  qo l  dnrd  que  sq  cmec  qd  utldrq ;
| |  |  |    | |      | |  |    |  | | | |        | |
otgoltqc  mrmc  ornnt  uletq  otqdstq  dqc  ltuqc
aussitot que vous aurez reçu cet avis, et
comptez que vous le recevrez probablement,
            |    ||| |  |        |  || |
sm. 2. lm. 3. ule otrrlled : ce dqc rrmtteqtc
|   || || ||                |        || |
dq ormmreqdo passer, le bruit omoder mrmc
|  | | |  |      ||| ||  |      |  ||        |
cdcotmetreo sq urd lttemqq qo mrmc uleteqc
|| | |      ||      | | | |
otqdstq dqc ltuqc cldc tqolts.
```

                                    " MARIE CAROLINE."
" 15 Avril, 1832."

Which being deciphered, stands thus in French:—

Je ferai savoir à Nantes, à Angers, et à Rennes, et à Lyons, que je suis en France; préparez vous pour faire prendre les armes aussitot que vous aurez reçu cet avis, et comptez que vous le recevrez probablement du 2 au 3 Mai prochain: si les courriers ne pouvait passer, le bruit public vous instruiroit de mon arrivée et vous feriez prendre les armes sans retard.

I will make known at Nantes, at Angers, and at Rennes, and at Lyons, that I am in France. Prepare to take arms as soon as you receive this intelligence, which you will probably do from the 2nd to the 3rd of May next. If the couriers should be unable to pass, public report will acquaint you with my arrival, and you will take arms without delay.

Marie Caroline.   April 16, 1832.

On the 21st of April following, the duchess signed the following commission, which she wrote entirely herself:—

I will accept and reward all services rendered to my son, and especially those of Lieutenant-Colonel François Tournier, whom I hereby appoint Colonel.
Marie Caroline.
Missa, April 21st, 1832.

On the same day she embarked on board of the steamer *Carlo-Alberto*, where she signed a second commission as follows:—

I promise to reward all services rendered to my son, and especially those of the *chef-de-bataillon* Chartier, whom I hereby appoint Lieutenant-Colonel.
Approved,
Marie Caroline.
April 23rd, 1832.

The steamer touched at Genoa, put again to sea on the same day, and on the 29th was off Marseilles. During the night of the 29th the insurrection was to have broken out in that city.

The weather was, however, unfavourable to landing upon the coast. There was a heavy swell, it blew very fresh, and an attempt to near the land anywhere except in the roadstead of Marseilles, would expose the vessel to great danger. The captain, nevertheless, offered the duchess to run the risk; but she formally objected to it, requesting only that a boat might be lowered, as she was resolved to attempt a landing on the coast.

For a considerable time the captain refused to comply; but it is a peculiarity in the character of the Duchess of Berri, to adhere more strongly to her resolutions when any opposition is offered to them; and, seeing the captain's resistance to her will, she gave peremptory orders to lower the boat The commander of the steamer had now no alternative but to obey. The vessel was freighted by Her Royal Highness, and was, therefore, under *controul*.

Moreover, the reasons she gave were sacred: she had, she said, herself fixed the hour for the insurrection, and she would not fail to be present at that hour; she would not be deterred from keeping her word by the fear of a danger which certainly existed, but was not insurmountable, and thus place the throne of her son in jeopardy, as well as the lives of those who were about to hazard all in her cause.

The captain, therefore, had the boat lowered; two persons entered it with the duchess: namely, M. de Ménars and General de Bourmont. The rowers took their seats, and the frail bark, separating from the steamer, disappeared between two mountains of water, then rose upon the top of a wave like a flake of foam.

CHAPTER 5

Secret Landing

It was by a miracle that so slight a vessel was able, during three hours, to resist so heavy a sea. The duchess on this occasion was what she always is in real danger—calm, and almost gay. She is one of those frail, delicate beings whom a breath would be supposed to have power to bend, and yet who only enjoy existence with a tempest either over their head or in their bosom.

At length the three adventurous passengers from the *Carlo-Alberto*, were landed. On the coast without being perceived, for night had begun to set in. Not daring to enter any house, they resolved to pass the night where they were. The duchess, having wrapped herself in a cloak, lay down Under the shelter of a rock, and fell asleep, while M. de Ménars and General Bourmont kept watch over her till daylight.

The first glance which the twilight allowed them to cast upon the city, satisfied the Duchess of Berri that her instructions had been followed. The white flag had replaced the tricolour upon the church of St. Laurent, and the alarm-bell, whose deep tones escaped from the old church, now vibrated fearfully through the air. It required almost the exertion of manual strength to prevent her from entering Marseilles. Her companions, however, succeeded in prevailing upon her to wait some short time longer.

Soon after, a numerous crowd was perceived pressing forward upon the esplanade of La Tourette, and looking towards the sea, to try to discover the steamer *Carlo-Alberto*; for a report had been spread through the city, that the Duchess of Berri and General Bourmont were on board of this vessel, and that the Regent and the Marshal were coming to second the legitimatist movement which had just been effected.

At eight o'clock the adventurous duchess and her companions heard the drums beating to arms in every part of the city. This continued till eleven, without any report of fire-arms being mingled with it; then all was again silent At nine, the tricolour flag had resumed its place upon the church of St. Laurent; at twelve, the crowd assembled on the esplanade of La Tourette, dispersed at the sight of the National Guard and the troops of the line, whose arms the duchess saw glittering in the sun's rays, upon the terrace.

At two in the afternoon, a frigate left the harbour, bearing the tricolour flag, and standing out under a press of sail. She rapidly approached the steamer, which then appeared about four leagues from shore, floating, like a buoy, upon the waves. The *Carlo-Alberto* on perceiving the frigate, seemed to arouse from her slumber; at first she began to move gently, as if in the act of awaking, then she suddenly started off with great speed, and soon disappeared in the direction of Toulon.

All these were unfavourable symptoms for the duchess and her companions. To have remained any longer where they then were, would have been the height of imprudence; General Bourmont, therefore, proposed to Her Royal Highness to enter a hut which they saw at a little distance, whilst he went on a journey of discovery. This hut belonged to a charcoal-burner.

At four o'clock, General Bourmont returned with the following intelligence: During the whole of the night of the 29th and the morning of the 30th, mobs of legitimates had assembled, and paraded through all parts of the city, carrying a white flag, and shouting, "*Vive Henri V.!*" At three in the morning, some armed men had entered the church of St. Laurent, after having obtained the keys by force, and had planted the white flag upon it in lieu of the tricolour. Other armed men had proceeded to the *Patoche* and to the watchhouse, had torn the tricolour flag from them, and had dragged it through the mud.

But by far the greater number of the insurgents had gone to the Palais de Justice, shouting, "*Vive la Ligue!*" "*Vive Henri V.!*"

A sub-lieutenant of the 13th, on duty there, summoned the crowd to disperse, and, on a refusal to comply made by its ringleader, Colonel de Lachaud, he seized the latter by the collar, and, after a violent struggle, dragged him into the guard-house. A general *"sauve qui peut"* was then heard, and during the rout three other individuals were taken: these turned out to be M. de Candolle, M. Laget de Podio, and M. Chevalier.

The patriotic feelings manifested by the majority of the population, and the little sympathy these legitimatist demonstrations had excited, was of bad augury for the success of the enterprise. Scarcely two hundred Carlists had taken a part in the movement, although there were six or eight thousand in the city; and it was probable that the other towns in the south would not rise unless Marseilles, their queen city, set them the example. This was disastrous intelligence, and the duchess and her little council eagerly consulted as to what was best to be done.

A determination of some kind was urgent, for their situation was very precarious, and the danger increased every moment To add to their misfortune, the disappearance of the *Carlo-Alberto* had cut off their retreat by sea, and they had, therefore, only a choice of two alternatives left: either to pass through the country separating the Rhone from the Alps, cross these mountains, and descend into Piedmont; or, turning westward, to cross France in nearly its whole breadth, and take shelter in La Vendée. This latter plan, though the most dangerous in its execution, had, at least, a chance of success in its result, and was, therefore, chosen by the duchess.

She declared, that since she had entered France, she would not leave it, and, with the rapidity always attendant upon her resolves, gave orders for immediate departure. She was desirous of taking advantage of the darkness of the night to make the first stage as long as possible. They had neither horse, nor mule, nor carriage; but the duchess declared that she was a very good walker. Nothing was now wanting but a guide; and the owner of the hut having offered his services, the mother of Henry V. replied by repeating her orders for instant departure.

The Duchess of Berri had a friend residing in the neighbourhood of Montpellier, upon whose fidelity and attachment she could depend.[1] It was therefore advisable to reach his house as soon as possible; but as the high roads were, no doubt, already guarded, and a woman and two men of the appearance of the duchess and her companions, travelling on foot, whether they journeyed by day or by night, could not possibly escape the attention of the police, Her Royal Highness asked the guide, if he knew of any road through the mountains, and on his replying in the affirmative, exclaimed, "Then lead the way."

The little party now left the sea-shore. The night was dark, and they could distinguish Marseilles at the other extremity of the bay, only by its numerous lights, which twinkled like stars. Now and then a murmur arose from the agitated city, and being carried forward by a low and humid current of air, reached the ears of the travellers.

Then the duchess would turn round, cast another parting glance towards the city of her lost hopes, and again resume her wearisome journey with a sigh. These symptoms of regret did not, however, last long; and no sooner had she lost sight of Marseilles, than she seemed to have forgotten her disappointment, and to think of nothing but the road, the difficulties and ruggedness of which increased with every step of her progress. The night was so dark, that the travellers could with difficulty see where they placed their feet; and in this way they walked on during five consecutive hours.

The guide then stopped; every trace of the pathway had disappeared, and the party found themselves in the midst of rocks, with a few stunted olive trees scattered here and there. The guide betrayed evident marks of indecision, and, on being questioned by the travellers, at length confessed that he had deviated from the path, the darkness having prevented him from following it, and that he knew not where they then were.

He begged he might be allowed to set out alone, and seek the path, promising to return for the duchess and her companions the moment he had found it. But as this man might possibly prove

1. My reasons for not naming this friend and his place of residence, may easily be conceived.

a traitor who had led them out of their road the more easily to betray them, General de Bourmont opposed his being allowed to depart. The duchess, on the other, hand, was so dreadfully tired, that she could walk no further. The preceding night had, however, seasoned her to the life of bivouac she was about to pursue; she therefore wrapped herself in her warm cloak, laid her head upon a portmanteau, and was soon as fast asleep as if she had been in her bed at the Tuileries. Meanwhile, her companions kept watch over her as well as over the guide.

At dawn of day the duchess awoke. The instant there was light enough, the guide discovered where he was. He had wandered two leagues from the path he ought to have followed, and to regain which, it was necessary to cross, for the space of a league, a tract of open country where they would run the danger of being recognized and taken. The duchess perceiving a country-seat at a little distance, asked to whom it belonged.

"To a furious republican," the guide answered; "and, what is more, he is *maire* of the commune of C———."

"Very well," replied the duchess, "conduct me thither."

Her companions looked at her with astonishment.

"Gentlemen," she said, in the tone of voice which she always assumes when her determination is irrevocable, turning towards them, and without giving them time to speak, "the moment is come when we must part. There is less danger for us separately than if we remained together. Monsieur de Bourmont, you shall receive my orders at Nantes; proceed thither, and wait there for me. Monsieur de Ménars, do you reach Montpellier; there I will let you know where I am. *Adieu*, gentlemen; I wish you a safe journey, and may God be with you!"

So saying, she gave them her hand to kiss, and took leave of them. They both withdrew, well knowing that remonstrance would be vain.

The duchess, on finding herself alone, repeated her order to the guide to conduct her to the house of the *maire*. In a quarter of an hour they were in the *maire's* drawing-room, and notice was given to the master of the house that a lady wanted to speak to him in private. He made his appearance in about ten minutes, and the duchess advanced to meet him.

"Sir," said she, "you are a republican, I know; but no political opinions can be applied to a proscribed fugitive. I am the Duchess of Berri,—and I am come to ask you for an asylum."

"My house is at your service, Madam."

"Your office enables you to provide me with a passport, and I have depended on your getting one for me."

"I will procure you one."

"I must tomorrow proceed to the neighbourhood of Montpellier; will you afford me the means of doing so?"

"I will myself conduct you thither."

"Now, Sir," continued the duchess, holding out her hand to him, "order a bed to be got ready for me, and you shall see that the Duchess of Berri can sleep soundly, even under the roof of a republican."

Next evening, the duchess was near Montpellier; she had travelled thither in the *maire's char-à-banc*, seated by his side. As soon as M. de Ménars had joined her, preparations were made for her departure. Her royal highness and M. de Ménars got into a *calash*; the Marquis de L——, wrapped up in a box-coat, took the coachman's seat; and the travellers, with regular passports, took the high road from Montpellier to Carcassone. They were to stay a day at Toulouse, whence they were to proceed, by way of Bordeaux, to a *chateau* situated in the neighbourhood of St. Jean-d'Angely, and belonging to a friend of the Marquis de L——, who answered for the fidelity of this friend, though the latter was not aware of the visit he was about to receive. It was from this *chateau* that the duchess was to give notice of her arrival to the legitimatists at Paris, and disseminate her first proclamations in La Vendée.

The security with which the duchess trailed from Montpellier to Toulouse, inspired her with such a feeling of confidence, that, on reaching the latter city, she resolved to devote the day of rest she purposed enjoying there to receiving visits from persons well known to be devoted to her person, just as she did during her stay there in 1828. She therefore made known her arrival to about five-and-twenty individuals, stating that she should hold a reception from three in the afternoon till eight in the evening.

This reception took place with the same form, and, thanks to an incidental circumstance, with almost the same publicity, I may say, as if it had occurred at the Tuileries.

The duchess, as we have before stated, had announced her arrival, and her intention of holding a reception, to the most noted legitimatists of Toulouse. Among these was an old maid, so indiscreetly garrulous that *Madame* thought it right, as a measure of precaution, to exclude her from sharing in the honour she intended to confer upon the others. This person learnt the arrival of the Duchess of Berri from one of her friends, who thought that she also had received an invitation, and through the same channel, she heard of the invitations sent to several individuals of her party.

She waited for hers until four o'clock; after which time, considering this voluntary forgetfulness of her, the cause of which she did not know, as a slight not to be overlooked, she could resist her feelings no longer, but, proceeding to the most frequented promenade of Toulouse, stopped everyone she knew, begging them to decide whether she had not just cause of complaint against the Duchess of Berri, who, though aware of her well known devotion to her cause, had nevertheless come to Toulouse, sent invitations to many persons, and forgotten to include her among the number.

These particulars, for the truth of which I can vouch, may seem incredible in a country where the secret-service money of the police amounts to three millions of *francs*.[2]

The Duchess of Berri left Toulouse the same night; continued her journey next day in an open *calash*; passed through Bordeaux without stopping; crossed the Dordogne at Cublac, and of descending as far as Blaye, passed close along the walls of that citadel, which she then little thought would one day become the place of her captivity. This was the direct road to the *chateau* inhabited by one of her friends; an expression invariably used by the duchess when she spoke of any of her party. She was accompanied in this journey only by M. de Ménars, and by the Marquis de L——, who served as

2. 120,000*l.*

49

her guide.

At eleven o'clock the same night, the carriage stopped at the gate of a *chateau*.

The Marquis de L—— left the coach-box, and rang at the gate with the violence of one not inclined to wait. The loudness of the ring, and the lateness of the hour brought out the master himself.

"It is I—de L——," said the Marquis on perceiving him; "open the gate quickly, for I bring you Her Royal Highness the Duchess of Berri."

The master of the house started back with surprise and dismay.

"The Duchess of Berri!" he stammered out "What, *Madame?*"

"Yes, she herself;—open the gate quickly."

"But you are not aware that I have twenty visitors in the house, all of whom are now assembled in the drawing-room, and —"

" Sir," said the duchess, opening the blinds of the carriage, "have you not by any chance a female cousin living fifty leagues from this place?"

"Yes, *Madame.*"

"Well then, open the gate, and introduce me to these twenty visitors as your cousin."

There was no replying to this; and the master of the house, who had only made these objections in his anxiety for the safety of the duchess, instantly opened the gate. The fair heroine now leaped from the carriage, put her arm under his, and proceeded towards the house.

Meanwhile the visitors, on perceiving the absence of their host, had most of them withdrawn to their bed-rooms, so that when the duchess entered with M. de Ménars and the Marquis de L——, she found, in the drawing-room, only the lady of the house and two or three persons with her. The introduction was therefore less awkward.

Next morning the duchess came down to breakfast, underwent her second introduction, and played her part of cousin so naturally that no one present had the least suspicion of her not being the person she represented. It fortunately happened that not one of the guests had ever seen her before.

On the following Sunday, the *curé* of the little commune of S——, to whose flock the inhabitants of the *chateau* belonged, came thither as usual to breakfast, and to him the duchess was introduced in the same manner that she had been introduced to the other guests, as the cousin of the master of the house. The *curé* gravely advanced towards Her Royal Highness to offer his respects, but stopped suddenly in the middle of the room, with such an air of stupefaction that the duchess burst out laughing.

The good priest had been presented to the Duchess of Berri, and had taken up an address to her, when she came to Rochefort in 1828. He seemed now to associate the features of the pretended cousin, with his recollections of Her Royal Highness.

"What is there in my cousin's countenance, that makes so strong an impression upon you?" said the master of the house.

"Why there is," said the *curé*, stammering; "this is *Madame*—your—cousin—oh! but it is really surprising."

"What is surprising?" said the duchess, much amused at the priest's embarrassment.

"There is that—your Royal Highness is like *Monsieur* ——'s cousin—I mean that *Monsieur* ——'s cousin resembles your Royal Highness. The fact is, I took you for—and even now—I could almost swear that ——"

The duchess laughed like a mad woman. At this moment the bell announced breakfast.

The duchess was seated at the breakfast-table opposite to the *curé* who, being still preoccupied by the strange resemblance, kept looking at the cause of his embarrassment, and forgot to eat; or if his absence of mind was mentioned to him, he would raise his fork to his mouth instinctively, and, immediately replacing it upon his plate, exclaim—"It is incredible!—never did such a likeness exist before."

CHAPTER 6

A Call to Arms

The duchess remained a week at this *chateau* without being recognized, or having any cause for apprehension. It was from this place that she wrote to her *partisans* at Nantes and in different parts of the western provinces, and acquainted her friends in the south with the state of things in La Vendée; urging them all to take courage, and conform to the instructions they would soon receive.

At the same time, she stated to them the particulars of her happy, though fatiguing journey through France. She also wrote a letter to the principal legitimatist chiefs at Paris, giving them notice that she was about to enter La Vendée, and promising in a short time to make known to them the measures she intended pursuing.

I do not give this letter textually, but it was much to the same effect as the following, which, on the 15th of May, she addressed to M. de Coislin.[1]

"Let my friends take courage; I am in France, and shall soon be in La Vendée. It is from thence you will receive my definitive orders, and they will reach you before the 25th instant. Get ready then; there has been nothing but mistake and error in the south.

I am satisfied with its preparations; it perform its promises. My faithful provinces in the west never fail in theirs. In a short time, all France shall be called upon to resume its ancient dignity and its ancient happiness.

1. It was seized at the Chateau de la Laslière

M. C. R.[2]
May 15,1832.

To this letter was joined the following list, containing the names agreed upon, under which the conspirators were to conceal their real names, and correspond with each other.

Guibourg, (Pascal.)
The Marshal, (Laurent.)
Madame, (Mathurine.)
Mauqillé, (Bertrand.)
Terrien, (Coeur-de-Lion.)
Clouet, (St. Amand.)
Charles, (Antoine.)
Cadoual, (Bras-de-fer.)
Cathelineau, (Le Jeune, or Achille.)
Charrette, (Gaspard.)
Hebert, (Doisseville.)
D'autichamp, (Marchand.)
De Coislin, (Louis Renaud.)

On the same day she sent to M. Guibourg a written order [3] to take arms; at the same time she issued the following proclamation, several hundred copies of which were printed by means of a portable press.

Proclamation by *Madame*, Duchess of Berri, Regent of France.
Vendeans, people of Britanny, and all ye inhabitants of the faithful provinces of the west:
Having landed in the south, I have not feared to cross France in the midst of danger, in order to accomplish a solemn promise, that of coming among my brave friends and sharing in their perils and their labours.
I am at length among this people of heroes. Open your doors to the fortunes of France; I will place myself at your head,

2. The letter is thus signed with initials.
3. The reader will see this order in a subsequent page, enclosed in a letter from M. Guibourg to M. de Coislin.

certain as I am of conquering with such men.

Henry V. calls upon you; his mother, the Regent of France, has devoted herself to your happiness: on some future day Henry V. will be our brother in arms, should the enemy threaten our faithful countries. Let us repeat our old, and our new cry, Long live the King! Long live Henry V!

Signed, Marie Caroline.

Royal Printing Office of Henry V.

The duchess was acting under a complete illusion with regard not only to the preparations in her favour but also to public feeling in the western departments. She compared these provinces to those in the south, which a simple proclamation might rouse into insurrection, and a single check as easily discourage. The people of La Vendée are grave, cold, and silent; they slowly and laboriously discuss every project, alternately weighing each chance of success and of failure. And when the former seems to preponderate in the balance, the Vendean holds out his hand, says yes, and dies if necessary in the fulfilment of life promise. But, as he knows that yes and no are to him words of life and death, he is slow in giving them utterance.

Thus also, when, in conformity to what she had stated to them in her letter of the 15th of May, the Duchess of Berri sent an order to the Vendean chiefs to take arms, she received on the 24th, even from those most devoted to her cause, answers which she was far from expecting. Of twelve the chiefs who were to command the twelve divisions of which Charrette was the *generalissimo*, seven protested against it in the name of their men, whom they sent to their homes; but declared that, so far as regarded their individual persons, their blood, under all circumstances, belonged to the duchess, and they were ready to shed it for her.

They trusted, however, that she surely would not assume before God and man the terrible responsibility of dragging their peasants into an attempt which would prove nothing but a sanguinary and useless piece of rashness, since La Vendée, reduced to its own means, had no other hope but to protract a civil war in four or five departments, which would thereby be cut off from all communication with the rest of France.

They who thus separated themselves from the cause of the Duchess of Berri, were termed "*Pancailliers*," from the name of a cabbage peculiar to the country, which rapidly grows to the height of three or four feet, and then proves abortive.

It seems that the Marquis de Coislin himself, whose promises had led the duchess into her present situation, had no greater influence over his subordinate chiefs than Charrette had over those he commanded; for, on the 17th of May, he sent her the following note in La Vendée, which she had entered on the 16th.

"The several orders transmitted, in the name of *Madame*, to the departments in the west, prove that Her Royal Highness has received from the emissaries sent by her, the most false reports on the real situation of those departments; and that these emissaries have stated to *Madame* absolutely the reverse of what they were instructed to tell her. Someone, therefore, whose veracity may be depended upon, must undertake to deliver to *Madame* the following note which contains the exact truth with regard to the western departments.

"The armament is far from being what it ought to be, to carry on the war with advantage. It consists of muskets landed upon the coast by the English during the former revolution, and also during the hundred days. The latter are alone fit for service, though many of them are nearly useless for want of care, and from the necessity the owners were under of concealing them, as well under the administration of De Cazes, as since the revolution of 1830.

"Moreover, some of the individuals who possessed such arms, have sold them, either for the sake of the price, or to exchange them for fowling-pieces. The present armament, therefore, consists only of old British muskets, and a pretty good number of fowling-pieces, which greatly increases the difficulty of issuing cartridges, particularly in action.

"There is still a greater deficiency of powder than of muskets. Since the revolution of 1830, we have not been able to procure it in our departments without the greatest difficulty, and even then only pound by pound.

"The *patroles* and domiciliary visits have necessitated the greatest precaution to prevent this powder from being discovered in the houses. It has been concealed in hollow trees, haystacks, piles of faggots, &c. &c. The damp has caused many serious losses in this commodity, and it must be candidly stated, because it is the truth, which must be made known to *Madame* and her advisers, that most of the divisions have not sufficient ammunition to carry on the war for the space of a fortnight.

"When we took up arms in 1815, we were in the same predicament; but at that period we depended, and had good reason to depend, upon the assistance of England, mistress of the sea, whilst at present we have nothing to hope. All the chiefs are aware of this state of things, so also are the faithful and devoted land-owners; and all of them well know that we cannot act with any hope of success unless supported by European armies, which, by attacking the frontiers of France, would force Louis-Philippe to withdraw from our departments a portion of the troops of the line now stationed there, and which are very numerous.

"They are likewise aware that it will be very difficult to form the first meetings, which even then would be far from numerous, because we all know that, as our enemies possess the resources of which we are deprived, it is impossible that the royalists alone can re-establish legitimacy. Everyone feels this impossibility; and if ill-advised orders, which we will nevertheless obey, should force us to take arms, we would call to our standard only a few men endowed with supernatural courage, and some others selected from among those who have nothing to lose.

"But if we do not assume arms until we are backed by foreign armies, our countries, and we may say it with truth, will rise almost in mass, and present a very formidable force; everyone being as firmly convinced that the revolution is not in a state to resist a coalition of Europe, as that without such coalition the royalists can do nothing. The great cities will not join us until they see that we are so supported; without that, they will be against us, whatever may be the feelings of their inhabitants, who would not rush into an undertaking which offered not the slightest chance of success.

"Let not *Madame* be dazzled, therefore, by the words, flattering no doubt, but devoid of probability, which are constantly dinned in her ears. France has now everything to hope; but it will have nothing, if we are made to take arms at the present juncture. If we act prematurely, a month will scarcely elapse before La Vendée will cease to exist; this last resource of the monarchy will be lost; all its chiefs will be either taken or killed, and the country entirely laid waste. If the fifty thousand troops in the western provinces were not sufficient to effect this, a greater number would soon be forthcoming, unless foreign war kept the army on the frontiers; in which case, part of the troops now opposed to us, must be called away. Fifty thousand regular troops, well supplied with arms and ammunition, are fearful odds against men in want of everything.

"A day will perhaps come, if it be patiently waited for, when everything may be done by France alone, without foreign aid, which would no doubt be infinitely preferable. But this day is not yet arrived. The wretchedness of the people in the great towns; during the next winter, may greatly hasten its approach; for, however powerful the exertions and encouragement in those towns, it will be impossible to supply the wants of the working classes, especially at the exorbitant price to which corn has risen in consequence of the bad crops. Would it not be better to make Louis-Philippe bear all the odium of this unavoidable misery, than to charge it upon Henry V. and the regency of *Madame*, even supposing a restoration might be effected before or during the winter?

"Nothing can henceforth prevent this state of wretchedness among the working classes from taking place; and if a restoration, or an attempt at a restoration, were now made, our enemies would tell the people that, if the restoration had not happened or not been attempted, all their wants would have been provided for; whilst, in the contrary case, we might, and with much greater reason, tell the workmen out of employment, the shopkeepers who sell nothing, and those who have become bankrupts, that it is solely to the glorious revolution,—to Philip, and to his government, that they are to impute their sufferings,—the royalists having left this king and his ministers to do as they pleased, without opposition.

"We beseech *Madame* to take these observations into consideration, and we intreat her not to give faith to those persons who have told her, concerning our countries, quite the reverse of what we had authorized them to tell her.

"An ill-timed attempt made by Holland has already prevented the overthrow of the Périer administration, and has even given it greater stability than it before possessed. The same result would attend every partial attempt, especially one made by the royalists, who in a moment would have all the revolutionary parties united against them, and would sever from their cause all those individuals who make up their minds upon the chances of success which they see,—such chances having really no existence at present, unless with the aid of foreign armies.

"An assumption of arms on our part without such aid, and in our present situation, would, as I have already stated, lead to nothing but the entire destruction of the royalist party. And what would be the consequence, if France, at any future period, were attacked by Europe? That there would then exist no royalist army to set forth the claims of Henry V.; that the foreign conquerors of the revolution might dispose as they pleased of our invaded provinces, without *Madame* being able to present to them her august son at the head of a devoted army, ready, if required, to maintain his rights over the whole of France.

"Let the matter therefore be duly weighed. The attitude of the western departments is great and noble, because they are feared. They are keeping fifty thousand regular troops in check. If *Madame* orders them to take arms, they will surely obey her order, but such a movement will only expose their want of resources. The masses will not rise for want of arms and ammunition, and more especially for want of confidence in an attempt, the sole idea of which appears extravagant to those aware of the real state of things, who know that, unprovided as we are, we can do nothing without foreign aid, but who, on the other hand, are well convinced that against such aid the revolution would be powerless.

"It was with a perfect knowledge of our situation that we charged the emissaries sent by *Madame* to intreat her not to make us assume arms for the cause of Henry V. until the first shots had been fired, on the frontiers, by the armies of Europe, or in the event of a complete anarchy at Paris, caused by the destruction of Philip and his family, or on the proclaiming of a republic,—events which may perhaps take place in the course of the ensuing winter, occasioned by the despair to which want may drive the working and industrious classes.

"We have, up to the present time, derived nothing but advantage from waiting; many people have had their eyes opened, and now perceive how greatly they have been duped. The increase of taxation produces a good effect, even in the interior of France; hence new levies of troops will encounter more opposition than former levies. Everything warrants our supposing, that, to succeed, we must evince patience and prudence, and, above all, not commit ourselves in future by ill-judged orders which must afterwards be recalled, and which, having been already given several times, have raised the persecutions to which we are exposed, and contributed, more than anything else, to the loss of ammunition which we have experienced."

The duchess replied to this note on the 18th. Her letter was forwarded to the Marquis de Coislin by M. Guibourg, who added to it a letter from himself, signed with his assumed name. It likewise enclosed the order for taking arms, given by the duchess on the 15th of May. The following is M. Guibourg's letter:—

Monsieur le Marquis,
I have the honour to enclose a textual and literal copy of the order which I am charged by her Royal Highness Madame, Duchess of Berri, to transmit to all the civil and military chiefs in the west.
copy.
In consequence of the reports addressed to me concerning the western and southern provinces, my intentions are that arms shall be taken on the 24th of this month (24). I have

59

everywhere made known my orders on this subject, and I transmit them this day to my provinces in the west.

Marie Caroline.

Saintonge, May 15th, 1832.

Since this order was given, *Madame*, Regent of France, has come to La Vendée, and I have had the happiness of seeing her there.   I am, Sir,

Your respectful servant,

Pascal, Civil Commissary.

P.S. I enclose you a letter from *Madame*: the two other papers are in lemon-juice.

The following letter from the duchess was, as I have before stated, a reply to the Marquis de Coislin's note.

I have reason to be grieved at the statements contained in the note you have sent me. You will call to mind, Sir, the contents of your own dispatches. It was those dispatches, as well as a duty I considered sacred, which induced me to trust myself to the well-known loyalty of these provinces. If I gave orders to take arms on the 24th, it was because I felt sure of your participation, and in consequence of positive notes from the south, and from divers other parts of France.

I should deem my cause for ever lost, were I obliged to fly from this country, which I shall naturally be forced to do unless arms be taken forthwith. I shall then have no resource left but to lament, far from France, my having relied too much upon the promises of those in whose favour I have braved every danger in order to fulfil mine. I must confess, that, deprived as I am of the counsels of *Monsieur le Marechal,* I feel great difficulty in coming to such a resolution without him. But I have the assurance that he will be at his post, if he is not there already.

I could have wished that the loss of his advice had been supplied by yourself; but time was pressing, and I therefore felt bound to make an appeal to your devotion and your zeal. The order sent throughout France to take arms on the twenty-fourth of this month remains, therefore, in full force for the west.

It now remains for me, sir, to call your attention to the army. It will insure our success; and it is our duty to use towards it all possible means of persuasion. You will therefore take care to disseminate my proclamations and ordinances two days beforehand; and you will not commit any act of hostility against it, until you have exhausted all means of conciliation. Such is my positive will.

P.S. I beg you will immediately forward this letter to the persons who signed that which you sent to me. I need not tell you, *Monsieur le Marquis*, how greatly I rely upon your devotion, of which you have already afforded me so many proofs, and which becomes so necessary in the present crisis.

Marie Caroline,

Regent of France.

Vendée, May 18th, 1832.

The Marquis de Coislin, on receiving this letter, hastened to execute the orders of the duchess. He accordingly wrote to his son the following letter, the date of which, though not marked, must be the 19th of May.

I send you, my dear Adolphe, a copy of the orders I have just received from *Madame*. She is in La Vendée, and has given orders, in every part of France where she has friends, to take arms on the 24th of this month. Lose no time therefore in making this known to your followers, and take immediate measures for seizing, at a moment's notice, upon all the resources which you know of in the country, and which I need not here enumerate.

I enclose in the letter, the order for *Coeur-de-Lion,*[4] in order that he may act simultaneously with yourself. Madame's orders are to disseminate, two days beforehand, her proclamations among the troops of your cantonments, who are not to be attacked unless they refuse the proposals which *Mad-*

---

4. Terrien.

ame makes to them in her proclamations. You must make known to them, that is to say to the non-commissioned officers and privates, that all who join you shall be admitted to form a regiment of guards, and shall, if they wish it, obtain their discharge at the end of the campaign. It appears that *Madame* founds her chief hope upon the defection of the troops.

The letter which I have received from *Madame* is dated yesterday, May 18th, from La Vendée,

Pray send me my horses, on the 22nd, at Madame Coutance's.

It was the reception of this letter which led to the nocturnal conference between M. Adolphe de Coislin and the officer of the 32nd, in the wood of Guenrouet.[5]

The same day, the Marquis de Coislin despatched similar orders to Terrien, Le Roux, and La Roche-Mace, his *chefs-de-bataillon*. It is useless to transcribe them, as they are a mere repetition of his letter to his son. Nevertheless, the letter addressed to Terrien contains a passage not in the others. It is as follows:—

Let everything that is put in requisition belonging to the royalists, or persons who think well, be estimated at a high rate, and the reverse with regard to the liberals.

La Roche-Macé replied, that he and his men were ready. During the interval between the Marquis de Coislin's letter and the answer of his *chef-de-bataillon*, the former had an interview with M. de Bourmont. The following is the letter written by the Marquis to La Roche-Macé after this interview.

I have received your answer, my dear La Roche, and I am the more rejoiced at your having sent it to me immediately, because I have to give you a piece of news that will please you. I have just seen Marshal Bourmont, who has arrived. He regrets that *Madame* did not delay the breaking out of the affair; 'but,' said he, 'it is now impossible to suspend the

---

5. See the report quoted, in chapter 3.

orders she has given, and we must therefore make a beginning, as specified.' The marshal desires that our first attempt should be upon Ancenis, where he passed the night, and which, he says, is not at all guarded. There is only one sentinel of the national guard. He wishes you to take the cannon you will find there. Try at all events to get possession of the muskets and ammunition which you think the place contains. You may, however, if you think fit, begin by disarming the smaller cantonments.

Although these orders were given by the Marquis de Coislin with that apparent confience which a commander must always appear to feel, real confidence was nevertheless very far from his mind. The letter here given, addressed to his son, and dated May 21st, shows his misgivings, which were justified by the event.

I wrote to you, my dear child, on my return, and acquainted you with what we had decided upon. You have not sent me the information I requested of you. I have since forwarded to you *Madame's* orders, but the accounts I receive concerning the chiefs of the divisions in La Vendée, and many other things besides, make me fear, and with too great reason, that the movement in this part of the country will only end in the capture of *Madame*, who has no other hope of success than in the defection of the troops, which is very uncertain.

If they do not join her she is lost, and all the countries which have risen in her favour will be ruined. The population of La Vendée has greatly cooled in its zeal from the failure of the rash attempt at Marseilles; and such of the chiefs as could previously depend upon two or three thousand men, can now only expect a hundred and fifty or two hundred.

Under such circumstances we must defer the rising for a day or two, and wait to see what will be done by the troops which are to be sent against *Madame*, whose presence in La Vendée is known at Nantes. All the troops have been ordered to this part of the country; we must therefore adjourn the movement from the 28th to the 30th. I write today to the district of Ancenis, and I enclose you a line for that of Chateaubriand, which you will forward.

I transmit you fresh orders in consequence of the news I have received from La Vendée. You will not send me my horses until I write to you for them. Many of our friends allege, as a reason for keeping back, that we were not to move except in the event of success in the south—instead of which everything has failed there; or in case we should receive assistance from foreign powers; or on the establishment of a republic.

Now, nothing of the kind has taken place. Let us therefore wait a few days; this will do no injury to our cause. In the mean time, send and ascertain what the department of Morbihan, said to be very lukewarm, is about. A knowledge of what is going on there may enable us to come to a decision:—you will let me know.

Meanwhile, the Duchess of Berri, as I have already stated, quitted on the 15th of May, at eleven o'clock, the *chateau* in which she had been so hospitably entertained, and entered La Vendée. She was to join M. de Charrette, on the next day, in the neighbourhood of Montaigu; and for this purpose she was obliged to travel the remainder of the day and the whole of the ensuing night. She was to stop half way at the house of a cure, who had received notice of her intended arrival from M. de Charrette, and who, zealously devoted to her party, had undertaken to have her conducted to the place of meeting. The duchess reached his house at about eight o'clock in the evening, attended only by her late host, as she feared that a greater number of attendants might excite suspicion. She had still seven leagues to travel.

As soon as the duchess had supped, she requested the *curé* to give the necessary orders for her departure, whilst she made her preparations. Both were soon ready; and when, at the expiration of a quarter of an hour, the priest returned to the room occupied by Her Royal Highness, to tell her that the horse was saddled, he found her dressed as a peasant-boy, bearing the appearance of a youth of eighteen. Her light auburn tresses were completely hid under a brown wig.

He then called his godson, a stripling of sixteen, and pointing to Her Royal Highness, said only these few words:

"Here is a young man who will get up behind you. He must be taken to ———.

The lad, casting a rapid glance at the person committed to his guidance, replied, "Very well, *Monsieur le Curé*, he shall be taken thither."

The duchess, having bid the good priest *adieu*, mounted behind her conductor, and the horse started off at a trot.

They travelled on without either party saying a word, and the guide did not once turn his head towards his companion. In three hours they reached the place appointed.

The disguised duchess having made herself known to the persons waiting to receive her, entered the house where she was expected. The lad who had brought her, immediately set out on his return, without saying a word to her or asking for any reward. At four o'clock he reached his godfather's residence.

"Well!" said the *curé* "Did you take the young man to the place of his destination?"

"Yes, *Monsieur le Curé*."

"And did you take good care that nothing happened to him?"

"Oh, certainly; for it was well worth while."

The young lad having seen the duchess in 1828, had recognised her even under her disguise. The character of the Vendean peasant is fully displayed in this action, so simple at a first view, and yet so characteristic. He is ever the same—cold, silent, and devoted.

Charrette arrived at the hour appointed. The duchess and he got on horseback to proceed to the neighbourhood of Grand-Lieu; and, after about an hour's travelling, an accident happened which had well nigh terminated the campaign ere it was begun.

In crossing the Maine a little below Remouillé on a bridge, or rather a dike of wet stones, the duchess's foot slipped and she was precipitated into the little river. Charrette immediately jumped in to the water and bore her to the opposite bank.

Our heroine who, as the reader must recollect, was dressed as a boy, had no change of clothes, which greatly embarrassed her; but, perceiving a house close by, she entered it, undressed, and going straight to a bed, took from it a blanket which she wrapped round her whilst her clothes were drying; then returning to the cheering rays of the sun outside the door of the house, partook of a bowl of sour milk and a piece of black bread, which her companions had asked for.

At Aigrefeuille, the duchess, having obtained the garments of her sex and a carriage, pursued the high road as far as Touffou, where she entered a house. A woman soon after left it dressed in her clothes, and entered the carriage, which continued to follow the road to Nantes. The duchess in the meantime, dressed in the clothes which the woman had exchanged for hers, took a cross road, and entered the most intricate part of the country. She thus hoped, should she have been followed, to put her pursuers upon a wrong scent.

On the same day, (17th) she stopped at a wretched cottage, but far from any other dwelling, and perfectly concealed from casual observation. Thence she made M. de Bourmont acquainted with her arrival in La Vendée. The general also had reached Nantes on the 17th, after travelling through France by way of Lyons and Moulins. There likewise the Duchess of Berri received the Marquis de Coislin's note and the visit of M. Guibourg.

CHAPTER 7

Perilous Journey

Whilst this was passing, the letters which the duchess had written to the royalists at Paris had reached their destination, and excited
great apprehensions in the persons to whom they were addressed.
A long despatch in cypher had accompanied the letter of advice,
and the duchess in a fit of absence had forgotten to send the key.
M. Berryer discovered it, and it consisted of the following phrase
substituted for the twenty-four letters of the alphabet: —

"Le gouvernement provisoire."

Though the persons to whom these letters were addressed were
all at Paris, they saw the real state of affairs much more clearly and
positively than the duchess did. They well knew that there was
no hope of success to be derived from Vendean revolts. On the
contrary, the proceedings of the ministers, according to their view,
would, by rendering the government more and more unpopular, afford
good chances and probabilities of success at some future period.
They therefore met on the evening of the 19th, to concert the
means of making known the true situation of France to the adventurous duchess.

It was accordingly agreed that one of them should proceed to
La Vendée and confer with Her Royal Highness. The difficulty
was to select this individual. From the suspicious vigilance of the
government, Messrs. Chateaubriand and Fitzjames were watched in
all their motions; they could not therefore advance a step towards La Vendée without betraying the secret of the cause. M.

Hyde de Neuville was similarly situated. M. Berryer, by using the pretence of a lawsuit which required his services, during the first days of June, at the assizes of Vannes, could alone attempt the mission with any prospect of success. He therefore proposed to take it upon himself, and stated the means by which he hoped to elude the vigilance of the police. His plan was approved of, and a note drawn up by M. de Chateaubriand, being a mere summary of the opinions of the meeting collectively. The remainder was left to M Berryer's zeal and eloquence.

M. Berryer left Paris on the morning of the 20th, and reached Nantes on the 22nd. On his arrival, he was informed that M. de Bourmont had been there for two days past He immediately paid the general a visit. M. de Bourmont had, on the 15th of May, received the order for taking arms on the 24th; but, after what he had heard during his short residence at Nantes, he thought, with M. Berryer, that no hope could be founded upon this insurrection, which he considered a lamentable piece of rashness and folly.

He was so strongly of this opinion that he had taken upon himself to send an almost counter-order to the Vendean chiefs, trusting that when he saw the Duchess of Berri he should succeed in making her renounce her project. This counter-order had been transmitted by M. Guibourg to the Marquis de Coislin, who was to send it to the persons whom it concerned. I here give M. Guibourg's letter, together with a copy of M. de Bourmont's order.

Monsieur le Marquis,
I have the honour to transmit herewith a copy of the order which I am directed to send you on the part of the Marshal.
Delay for some days the execution of the orders you have received for the 24th of May, and let no overt act take place until you receive further orders; but continue your preparations.
Marshal, Count de Bourmont.'
May 22nd, 13 o'clock at noon."

M. de Bourmont applauded the motive which had led M.

Berryer to seek an interview with the duchess, and all was ready for his departure on the same day. Accordingly, at two o'clock in the afternoon, M. Berryer got into a small hack cabriolet, and, as he entered it, asked the duchess's confidential agent at Nantes, what road he was to take, and where she resided. The agent replied by pointing to a peasant at the corner of the street, mounted on a dapple-grey horse, saying:—"Look at that man;—you have only to follow him."

In fact, no sooner did the peasant perceive the cabriolet in motion than he trotted forward, so that M. Berryer could follow without losing sight of him. In this manner they crossed the bridges and entered the open country. The peasant never once turned his head towards the person he was guiding, but jogged on with such apparent carelessness and inattention, that M. Berryer more than once thought himself the dupe of some mystification. With regard to the cabdriver, as he was not in the secret, he could give no information about the road they were pursuing; and when, on his asking whither he was to drive, his fare had merely replied, "Follow that man," he strictly obeyed the injunction, and took no more notice of the guide than the latter took of him.

After a journey of two hours and a half, during which M. Berryer felt considerable uneasiness, they arrived at a small town, and the peasant on horseback stopped in front of the only inn it contained, and alighted. The cab immediately drew up at the same place, and M. Berryer got out. The peasant then continued his journey on foot, and M. Berryer, having told the cab-driver to wait for him there till six o'clock the next evening, instantly followed his strange guide.

Having advanced about a hundred yards, the guide entered a house; and as during this short walk M. Berryer had gained upon him, he followed close at his heels. The man opened the door of the kitchen, where the mistress of the house was alone, and pointing to M. Berryer, who was close behind him, said:—"Here's a gentleman who must be conducted."

"He shall be conducted," replied the mistress of the house.

No sooner had she uttered these words than the peasant opened a door and disappeared, without giving M. Berryer time to thank or remunerate him. The mistress of the house then made the stranger a sign to be seated, and continued, without saying a single syllable, to attend to her household fairs, as if she were alone.

A silence of three-quarters of an hour succeeded the sole mark of politeness which M. Berryer had received, and was only interrupted by the arrival of the master of the house, who bowed to the stranger without evincing either surprise or curiosity; only he looked towards his wife, and the latter, without stirring from her place, and without interruption to what she was doing, repeated the words previously uttered by the guide—"Here's a gentleman who must be conducted."

The master of the house then cast upon his guest one of those rapid, uneasy, and searching glances peculiar to the Vendean peasantry; after which, his countenance resumed its habitual expression, of kindness and *naïveté*. Advancing towards M. Berryer with his hat in his hand—

"Does *Monsieur* wish to travel in our country?" he asked.

"Yes, I wish to go further on."

"*Monsieur* has papers, no doubt?"

"Yes."

"In regular order?"

"Perfectly."

"If *Monsieur* would show them to me, I would inform him whether he could with safety travel through our country."

"Here they are."

The peasant taking them, glanced his eye over their contents; and the moment he saw the name of Berryer, folded them up and returned them, saying:

"Oh! it's all right. *Monsieur* may go anywhere with these papers."

"And will you undertake to have me conducted?"

"Yes, Sir."

"I wish it to be as soon as possible."

"I will have the horses saddled immediately."

The master of the house then went out, and, returning ten

minutes after, said: "The horses are ready."

"And the guide?"

"Is waiting, Sir."

At the door, M. Berryer found a lad belonging to the form already on horseback, holding a second horse by the bridle; and the moment the foot of the Paris advocate was in the stirrup, the new guide, as silent as his predecessor, began to jog on.

In about two hours, during which M. Berryer did not exchange a single word with his guide, they arrived, about nightfall, at the door of one of those farmhouses honoured by the appellation of *chateaux*. It was now half-past eight. M. Berryer and his conductor both alighted, and entered the house.

The latter, addressing a servant, said:

"Here's a gentleman who must speak to your master immediately."

This latter was already in bed. He had passed the preceding night at a rendezvous, and the whole of the day on horseback. Being therefore too tired to get up, one of his relations came down in his stead.

The moment M. Berryer stated who he was, and that he wished to see the Duchess of Berri, orders were instantly given to prepare for their departure, the host's relative undertaking to conduct the traveller.

In ten minutes, both were on horseback. After a quarter of an hour's riding, a loud cry was uttered about a hundred yards before them. M. Berryer started, and inquired what that cry was.

"It is our scout," calmly replied the Vendean chief, "who, in his way, is asking whether the road is free. Listen, and you will hear the reply."

At these words he extended his hand, seized M. Berryer's arm, and thus forced him to pull up. An instant after, a second cry was heard, much further off than the former, of which it seemed an echo, so perfectly similar was the sound.

"We may now advance," resumed the chief, walking his horse forward; "the road is free."

"Are we then preceded by a scout?" asked M. Berryer.

"Yes, we have a man two hundred yards in advance of us, and

one two hundred yards in our rear."

"But who replied to the former?"

"The peasants whose cottages border upon the road. Take notice when we pass before one of them, and you will see a small wicket opened and a man's head appear through it, remain for an instant motionless, as if it were a statue, and only disappear when we have passed the house. If we were soldiers belonging to some neighbouring cantonment, the man who should see us pass would immediately go out by a backdoor; and if there were some meeting in the neighbourhood which we were going to surprise, it would receive notice of our approach a quarter of an hour before our arrival."

At this moment the Vendean chief ceased speaking. "Listen," said he, stopping his horse.

"What is the matter?" inquired M. Berryer; "I heard only the cry of our scout."

"Yes, but no cry replies to it;—there are soldiers in the neighbourhood."

So saying, he set off at a trot, and M. Berryer followed him; almost at the same moment they were overtaken by the man in the rear, who advanced at full speed.

Here the road branched off in two directions, and they found their scout motionless and undecided between the two paths. His cry had been answered on neither side, and he knew not which to take; for both led to the place whither the travellers were bound.

The chief and the guide having conversed together an instant in an undertone, the guide took the dark avenue to the right, and was soon lost in the gloom. Five minutes after, the chief and M. Berryer entered the same road, leaving their fourth companion motionless at the place they quitted, and, in five minutes, he followed them in his turn.

About three hundred paces from the meeting of the two roads, they found their guide at a dead stand. Having made them a sign to keep silence, he whispered these words, "A *patrole*."

And in fact they heard immediately afterwards the regular cadence formed by the footsteps of a body of soldiers marching. This happened to be one of my moveable columns going the night round.

The noise soon came nearer, and they perceived the bayonets of the men standing out in relief upon the dark sky. The detachment, however, to avoid the water running in the hollow roads, had taken neither of the two paths which had caused a momentary hesitation in the guide, but had climbed the slope, and were marching on the other side of the hedge, upon the ground commanding the hollow path which formed its boundary. The situation of the travellers was now very critical; for, if one of the four horses had neighed, the whole party would have been made prisoners. But, as if the poor beasts had understood the danger of their masters, they remained still and silent, and the soldiers marched on without suspecting near whom they had passed. When the sound of their footsteps had died away, the travellers resumed their journey.

At half past ten, they turned off from the road, and entered a small wood, where they alighted, and, leaving their horses under the charge of the two peasants, M. Berryer and the Vendean chief continued their route on foot

They were now not very far distant from the farmhouse inhabited by the Duchess of Berri; but, as they wished to enter by a backdoor, it was necessary to make a circuit, and cross a marsh, in which they sank up to their knees in mire. At length they perceived a little dark mass, which was the farm-house surrounded by trees. They soon reached the door, and the chief knocked in a particular manner.

Footsteps were immediately heard inside, and a voice exclaimed, "Who's there?"

The chief replied by a known password, [1] and the door was opened.

An old woman performed the duties of porter, but for greater

---

1. From delicacy, perhaps, to the Duke of Orleans, General Dermoncourt has not published this password; but as it may elicit a smile from our fair readers who Bare seen, in this country, the young and gallant heir to the French throne, we here insert it. The password was *Grand-Poulot*, a nickname given to the Duke of Orleans. It is not translatable. It bears, however, pretty nearly the same meaning as great baby, but is much more bitter; and it conveys besides, an imputation of chicken-heartedness. Let it be remembered, however, that this nickname, as applied to the Duke of Orleans, could have originated only in the warped imagination of a Carlist.—Tr.

security she was attended by a stout and robust peasant armed with a long and heavy stick, a weapon of terrific power in such hands.

"We want to see Monsieur Charles," said the chief.

"He is asleep," the old woman replied; "but he gave orders to be immediately informed if any one arrived. Come into the kitchen, and I will go and awaken him."

"Tell him that it is M. Berryer from Paris."

The old woman left them in the kitchen, and they approached the huge fire-place, in which were still some burning embers, the remains of the fire used during the day. One extremity of a board was in the fireplace, whilst at the other there was a slit containing one of those lighted pieces of pine which, in the Vendean cottages, are used as torches in lieu of lamps or candles.

In about ten minutes she returned, and informed M. Berryer that Monsieur Charles was ready to receive him. He accordingly followed her up a rickety staircase outside the house, which seemed scarcely fastened to the wall. It led to a small room on the first floor, the only one in the house at all fit to be inhabited.

This was the apartment of the Duchess of Berri, into which the old woman ushered M. Berryer, shut the door, and returned to the kitchen.

All M. Berryer's attention was now directed to the Duchess, who was in bed, upon a wooden bedstead clumsily made with a hedging-bill. She had sheets of the finest lawn, and was covered with a Scotch shawl of green and red plaid. She had on her head one of those woollen coifs worn by the women of the country, the pinners of which fall over the shoulders. The walls of the room were bare, the apartment was warmed by an awkward stove of plaster of Paris, and the only furniture, besides the bed, was a table covered with papers, upon which were two brace of pistols, and in a corner, a chair, upon which lay the complete dress of a peasant boy, and a black wig.

I have already stated that the object of M. Berryer's interview with the duchess was to persuade her to quit France; but, as I cannot give the particulars of this conversation without introducing, into matters of general interest, such as might prove injurious to private individuals, I shall pass it over in silence. The reader, with the details we have already given, may easily supply this deficiency. At three o'clock in the morning, but not until that hour, the Duchess of Berri yielded to the arguments urged by M. Berryer, both in his own name and in that of his party. Nevertheless, though she might easily have convinced herself that very little advantage could be expected from an armed insurrection, it was not without tears and cries of despair that she gave up the point.

"Well, it is settled," she said; "I must quit France; but I will not return, you may depend upon it; for I will not come back with foreign armies. They are only waiting, as you well know, for a proper time; then, when the day comes, they will demand my son. Not that they care much more about him than they did about Louis XVIII. in 1813; but he will prove a means of their having a party at Paris. Well! but they shall not have my son; they shall not have him upon any consideration. I would rather he should labour in the mountains of Calabria. Look you, M. Berryer; if he is to purchase the throne of France by the cession of a province, of a city, of a fortress, of a house, nay, of a poor cottage such as I now inhabit, I give you the word of a Regent and a mother that he shall never be king."

At four o'clock, the duchess seemed completely resigned, and M. Berryer took leave of her, having received her promise, that at noon she would meet him at the second house he had entered on the preceding evening, and which was four long leagues from the inn where he had left his cabriolet. On their arrival at this latter place, she was to enter this vehicle, return with him to Nantes, take the post there with a false passport, and, after crossing the whole of France, leave it by Mount Cenis.

M. Berryer stopped at the place appointed and waited from twelve till six in the afternoon, when he received a dispatch from the duchess, informing him that she had changed her mind.

She stated that she had linked too many interests with her own to fly from the consequences of her entrance into France, and to allow them to weigh upon others; that she was therefore resolved to share, to the very last extremity, the fate of those whom she had brought into peril; only the assumption of arms, fixed for the 24th of May, was adjourned to the 3rd and 4th of June. In consternation M. Berryer returned to Nantes.

On the 25th, M. de Bourmont received a letter from the duchess, confirming the one Digitized by she had written to M. Berryer. It is here subjoined.

Having come to the firm determination of not quitting the western provinces, but of trusting myself to their long tried fidelity, I depend upon you, my good friend, for the adoption of every necessary measure for the assumption of arms in the night between the 3rd and the 4th of June. I call all men of valour to my standard; God will aid us in saving our country; no danger, no fatigue shall discourage me; I will appear at the very first meetings.

Marie Caroline,
Regent of France.
Vendée, May 25th, 1832.

On the receipt of this letter, M. de Bourmont wrote to the Marquis de Coislin in the following terms:—

Madame having formed the courageous resolution of not quitting the country, but of calling to her all who are willing to concur in preserving France from the misfortunes which threaten it, makes known to all the Vendean chiefs that arms are to be taken on Sunday, the 3rd of June. Let them, therefore, meet on the following night, to act in concert, conformably to the directions you have given, Take care to ascertain that your notices have every where reached their destination.

Marshal, Count de Bourmont.

Such is the manner in which the Duchess of Berri reached La Vendée, and such is the cause of the movement denounced by M. de Chierre, and expected to take place on the 25th of May, being deferred till the night between the 3rd and 4th of June.

CHAPTER 8

Exposed!

The presence of the Duchess of Berri in La Vendée, by ceasing to be a secret, gave a more serious character to the civil war; and consequently, my precautions were increased, and my orders more severe. The small number of troops under my command did not allow of my reinforcing my cantonments, some of which were composed of only thirty, forty, or fifty men.

I was always, therefore, apprehensive of some of these posts being carried; and I gave strict orders, that, at night, the whole of the men composing each, should assemble in one place, and, on the very first attack, intrench themselves in the churchyard of the village they were in, as being the most favourable spot for making a stand.[1]

But there was something more to do than to provide against being surprised by the rebels: namely, to seize the persons of their chiefs. M. Dudoré had been already apprehended and conveyed to Nantes. His entrance into that city had nearly caused a riot; for the people, tired of the civil war excited during the two last years by the nobles, wanted to kill him. Ferraud and Petit-Pierre, the town-adjutants by whom he was escorted, had great difficulty in taking him to the prison; and it was not without imminent danger to themselves that they crossed the city. The mob talked seriously of throwing the carriage, with the prisoner in it, into the river; and the courage of the two town-adjutants certainly saved M. Dudoré's life.

1. See Appendix, Nos. 5. and 10.

This arrest produced so good an effect, by showing that the *chateaux* of the nobles were not inviolable,[2] as had hitherto been supposed, that I begged General Solignac to authorize my making another attempt of the same kind. Several reports had been made to me, representing the *chateau* of La Chaslière as the centre of the operations of the Vendeans.

Colonel de Laubépin, and his brother the military sub-intendant, had been described to me as the most ardent and most devoted among the Vendean chiefs. It therefore appeared to me advisable to take advantage of the adjournment of the day for taking arms, the reasons for which I was then ignorant of, and disorganize the movement, if possible, before it took place. Moreover, the Duchess of Berri might herself be there, and if so, I should at once put an end to the war.

These reasons did not, however, satisfy General Solignac, for he immediately declined authorizing me to undertake the expedition; and his repugnance to so rigorous a measure was so great, that, being almost forced by public clamour to yield to my representations, he quitted Nantes for Angers, leaving to the prefect and myself the care of directing this operation, the result of which was of such importance.

Accordingly, after having secured myself by procuring a warrant, I took my measures to prevent the inhabitants of La Chaslière from escaping. On the 26th, three detachments received orders to fall in at nine o'clock in the evening. At ten they began their march: the first advanced by Carquefou, the second crossed the Erdre at Sucé, and the third crossed the same river opposite Nais. Meanwhile, I myself marched, with an escort of twenty-five *gendarmes*, commanded by an officer named Rougon, and at the head of a company of grenadiers, towards Chapelle-sur-Erdre, by the road to Rennes. But the night being very dark, my guide had scarcely left the high road before he lost his way.

Towards four in the morning we reached Chapelle-sur-Erdre. This was one of the Rogation days, and there were men enough assembled in the public square to form a noble battalion, even with its

2. See Appendix No. 6.

full complement. I passed in the midst of them, and as I had dismissed my first guide, I called for another; but not a man would serve me. I therefore proceeded to the office of the *maire's adjunct*, and summoned him to accompany me. The poor devil obeyed much against the grain; for he feared that, on his return to the village, he should be murdered. But as he had no alternative but implicitly to obey my orders, I placed him in front of the column, and we proceeded on our march. Three-quarters of an hour after, we reached La Chaslière; but, being a good hour and half behind time, I found when I arrived, the *chateau* invested by my detachments.

I was then informed that my soldiers had been near apprehending two individuals, one of whom was just getting on horseback, and had escaped only by leaving his horse and portmanteau behind him. The other had returned to the *chateau*, pursued by one of my *voltigeurs*; but, the door being immediately closed after him, my men, who were the slaves of discipline, had waited for my arrival before they proceeded further:—and, in fact, I was the bearer of the only warrant which gave legality to the domiciliary visit I was about to make.

We entered the *chateau* without loss of time, and our search immediately commenced.

For a whole hour it was fruitless; but at length a man, with nothing on but his shirt and trowsers, was brought before me. He had been found in a secret recess, with a pistol in each hand. He informed me that he was the master of the house, and that his name was M. de Laubépin.

As we were disputing with him about the rank he held in the rebel army, a grenadier came into the room with three bottles in his hands.

"General," said he, with a somewhat embarrassed air, probably caused by a consciousness of the motive which had led him to the cellar, "here are some bottles which have a very seditious appearance."

"How so?"

"General, allow me to establish a fact: bottles are intended to hold wine, and sometimes other liquors, are they not?"

"Yes."

"Well, then," said the man, holding the bottles near my eyes, "there is no wine in them, nor spirits either, but papers."

I immediately perceived, by the looks of the master of the house, that this discovery by no means pleased him; and my curiosity was excited still more. Having broken the bottles, I found the letters, memoranda, and notes, written in cypher, some of which the reader has already seen in a preceding chapter, and which explained so minutely the military operations already effected by the rebel party, and those which remained to be performed.

Among these papers was a commission conferring upon M. de Laubépin the title of Intendent-General of the armies of the West. This came very seasonably, to put an end to our discussion as to the rank he held; and M. de Laubépin, probably considerng himself beaten, said not a word more.

Meantime, Madame de Laubépin was , made acquainted with the arrest of her husband and the discovery of the correspondence. This raised such serious alarm in her mind, that she sent to beg I would come to her apartment.

She was in bed, to which she was confined by a milk fever, consequent upon her accouchement which had just taken place. The poor woman was much affected; she thought her husband was to be shot immediately, without any other form of trial than what had just occurred.

I consoled her in the best manner I was able, and told her she had nothing of the kind to fear; that her husband would be taken to Nantes, where not a hair of his head should be hurt; that, with regard to herself, she might depend upon every kindness and attention to which a woman is entitled. When I left her, therefore, she was tolerably composed.

Having given orders for our departure, we were about to begin our march back to Nantes, when a sub-lieutenant of the 32nd approached me.

"General," said he, "will you allow me to offer you a single observation?"

"Willingly, Sir."

"There is a report that a lady is in the *chateau*, and that she is the Duchess of Berri."

"No, Sir, that is not the case. There is a lady in the *chateau* whom I have seen; but she is Madame de Laubépin."

"Pardon me, General; but you must be aware of the heavy responsibility you are under. Now, if Madame de Laubépin should disappear, pray consider what might be said."

I thanked this brave young man, and reflected that my enemies might take advantage of such a circumstance. The sequel has proved that I was right. But I thought I ought not, under any pretence, to remove Madame de Laubépin, in her present situation. I therefore directed my three detachments to continue to surround the house, and accompanied only by my grenadiers and my *gendarmes*, set out for Nantes with my prisoner, whom I placed near my person, and with the autograph papers, which I placed in my holsters.

Nevertheless, I took another road back, and proceeded towards Sucé, not caring to meet a second time the eight hundred men whom I had seen assembled at Chapelle-sur-Erdre, or to pass through the little wood which skirts that village; for, as I went by in the morning, I had remarked that five-and-twenty men in ambuscade there might attack three hundred with advantage, and my little body did not exceed fifty. I knew moreover that the inhabitants of Chapelle-sur-Erdre were, perhaps, of all the Vendeans, the most devoted to the cause of legitimacy; and yet their taxes were very regularly paid, there being not a single defaulter among them—a fact difficult to reconcile with their known political opinions. They are the handsomest and most powerful peasants I ever saw; and it was in this district that the first regiment of the royal guard, under the command of Colonel de Laubépin, was to have been raised.

On reaching Sucé, I halted and had refreshment given to my men, who had taken nothing since eight o'clock the previous evening, and it was then one in the afternoon. We resumed our march immediately after. At Carquefou I pressed forward in advance of the detachment, accompanied by only two *gendarmes*, and at six in the evening I was at Nantes.

My first care was to send a carriage to meet my prisoner, in order that he might enter the city without fear of ill-usage. This arrangement, which I considered my first duty, being made, I was preparing to call upon General Solignac, when he entered my house; the news of my arrival, and the capture I had made, having already reached him.

I handed over to him the correspondence I had seized, and we both went and deposited it with M. de Saint-Aignan. This form having been gone through, I retired to rest, for I was overwhelmed with fatigue. Meantime, General Solignac, from the information I had given him, drew up a *procès-verbal*, which I had not thought proper to do at La Chaslière, lest I should be surprised, with the few men I had there, by some party of Chouans, and not only my prisoner taken from me, whom I cared but little about, but the correspondence I had seized, for which I cared a great deal.

General Solignac, however, in drawing up this *procès-verbal*, committed an error both in law and in fact; for he dated the instrument from La Chaslière, although it was written at Nantes; and he affixed his own signature to it, though, at the time it was supposed to have been drawn up, he was at Angers. This trifling error, the motive of which is easily guessed, if the important result I had just obtained be taken into consideration, was more successful with the government than with the court of assize at Blois; for, thanks to this *procès-verbal*, the government gave General Solignac the praises that were due to me, whilst the assize-court, applied the term "forgery" to this document. I was forced, even at that period, to give to the jury the same explanation that I give here, in order to get this harsh term changed into that of "irregular." The error being rectified, I could not help admitting that it was one of the greatest "irregularities" that a commander-in-chief could commit.

The documents seized at the *chateau* of La Chaslière, some of which the reader is already acquainted with,[3] naturally lead to reflections very just indeed, but very galling to M. de Montalivert, upon the *Carlo-republican* alliance, every clue to which that minister, on the 6th of June, boasted of holding, though they es-

3. See the remainder in the two last numbers of the Appendix.

caped him on the 7th, and he has never been able to seize them since. And, indeed, it appears by the journey of M. Berryer to La Vendée—a journey which had no other object than to prevail upon the Duchess of Berri to leave France—as well as by the letter from the duchess to M. de Bourmont, containing the order to adjourn to the 4th of June the assumption of arms previously fixed for the 24th of May, that all these movements were far from being concerted with the republicans.

Even the coincidence of the affair of St. Méry with that at the *chateau* of La Pénissiere, upon which the minister of the interior dwelt so strongly, is naturally destroyed by the letter from the duchess, who, when she wrote on the 22nd of May, could not have guessed that General Lamarque would die on the 3rd of June, or that his military funeral would receive the bloody honours of the cannonading at St. Méry. Thus, there was no alliance between the two movements; there has been only a resemblance in the results: that is to say, in La Vendée, as at Paris, young men unaccustomed to the use of arms, defended themselves for a whole day against regular troops, thirty times more numerous than they were, and at length, when they could defend themselves no longer, they died—ay, by my faith, and nobly died!

It is a sad and lamentable thing to see such men, all of them the purest, bravest, and most devoted in a party, swept from the face of the earth by the scourge of civil war, for the particular interests of kings and rulers, whilst in foreign countries they might, with their talents and valour, have performed wonders for the general interests of their country. What would Charrette not have achieved against an enemy, when with a few badly armed peasants he kept in check our best generals and our best troops? What likewise would not Jeanne have effected against Russian or Austrian troops, when with ten men only he passed through a whole regiment of Frenchmen?

In delivering to General Solignac the documents I had seized, I communicated to him the doubts which had been raised with regard to the identity of Madame de Laubépin, stating also the necessity for placing my responsibility beyond impeachment by determining such identity. This time he agreed with me, and gave orders that the steamboat which performs the public service upon the Erdre, between Nantes and Nort, should be got ready, and well aired.

Next evening, at ten o'clock, the *marechal-de-camp* in command of the department, the *prefect*, the counsellors of *prefecture*, the president of the civil tribunal, the *procureur du roi*, and his officers, the colonel of *gendarmerie*, the *chef-d'escadron*, the colonel-commandant of the national guard, his *chefs-de-bataillon* and adjutant-major, Colonel Simon Lorrière, the town-major, the *maire* of Sucé, and a garrison of fifty grenadiers and *voltigeurs*, went on board the steamboat, whither I accompanied them. There remained no military authority at Nantes but the colonel of the 32nd, whom General Solignac had probably been unable to find, and no civil authority except the *juge de paix* and his registrar. At a quarter past ten, the boat glided majestically through the stream, offering the Chouans a fine opportunity for revenge.

At eleven o'clock we stopped for an instant, and not without risk of grounding, at the estate belonging to the *maire* of Sucé, which we were obliged to cross to get into the arm of the Erdre leading to La Chaslière, itself standing in the middle of a small peninsula, and in a most picturesque situation. At length the whole merry cargo of authorities, civil and military, landed at a quarter of an hour's walk from this *chateau*.

The noise we made was heard by the little garrison of La Chaslière, who, mistaking us for a party of Chouans, immediately got under arms. My orders for observing the most active vigilance had been strictly followed; for the officer commanding the detachment was well aware that, situated as he was at a distance from all assistance, his life would have been in danger had he neglected them.

Moreover, Colonel de Laubépin, whom we had been unable to apprehend, was in the neighbourhood, and everyone knew him to be capable of making a desperate attempt upon La Chaslière. General Solignac, on our landing, took all the military precautions so necessary, especially at night, in a place where the localities are unknown. For my own part, as I was well acquainted with them, I went on in advance of the rest of the party, accompanied by Colonel Simon Lorrière; but we were soon stopped by the challenge of an advanced sentinel. We looked at each other in great embarrassment, as neither of us knew the countersign. A second challenge reached us, and at the same moment we heard the sentry cock his piece. I hastened to reply "General Dermoncourt." The sentry then called out to his corporal, and we reached the *chateau* a quarter of an hour before the rest of the party.

In the apartments on the ground-floor, we found all the garrison in a bustle and under arms, expecting every moment to be attacked. Their surprise was, therefore, great when I appeared among them. I immediately announced the visit of General Solignac, and the men went out to pay him the usual military honours.

Meanwhile, I proceeded towards the apartment of Madame de Laubépin, who was still confined to her bed. It was impossible to advance a step in the corridors and antechambers without stumbling over mattresses; for the whole *chateau* had been converted into a vast bivouac. I found Madame de Laubépin tolerably composed in the midst of all this bustle and noise; and if she still felt any uneasiness, the information I gave her respecting the arrival of her husband at Nantes, and the precautions I had taken to preserve him from all accidents, must have completely dispelled it. When I saw that she was quite calm, I gave her notice of the visit she was about to receive, and requested she would dress herself. This she instantly complied with, notwithstanding her state of extreme weakness; and she had scarcely completed her toilet before General Solignac and his staff made their appearance.

General Solignac acquainted Madame de Laubépin with the mistake that had been made regarding her, at which she could not help smiling, especially when she saw the stir that this mistake had caused among the authorities at Nantes. She then called upon the *maire* of Sucé, to whose jurisdiction she belonged, to declare whether or not she was the Duchess of Berri.

The identity of the lady being fully proved in the presence

of every individual composing the party, General Solignac gave her a piece of news which seemed to afford her considerable pleasure: it was, that at daybreak she would be relieved from the presence of her garrison. He further advised her to proceed to Nantes, if she thought the state of her health would allow it. for the purpose of giving assistance and consolation to her captive husband.

We then took leave of her, and the party, being perfectly satisfied, returned to the steamboat. At two in the morning we reached Nantes. Notwithstanding a constant and heavy rain, we found the garrison under arms, and the whole population assembled at the port. A report had been spread that the Duchess of Berri had been arrested at the *chateau* of La Chaslière, and each expected to see her arrive.

The important result of my expedition to La Chaslière, induced General Solignac and the prefect to determine upon another expedition of the same kind to the *chateau* of Carheil, inhabited by the Marquis and Marchioness de Coislin. I therefore directed Commandant de Savenai to proceed, on the 30th of May, to this *chateau*, after combining the time of his arrival there with that of my own. I accordingly left Nantes on the day specified, with a company of *voltigeurs* and twenty-five moveable *gendarmes*; and I had so well taken my measures, that, at the very moment I arrived by one road, I perceived Commandant de Savenai with his detachment approaching in an opposite direction.

The *chateau* stands in an excellent situation for defence: it is surrounded on all sides by very thick and magnificent woods; these might be filled with *tirailleurs* in ambuscade, to defend the approaches to the house. And indeed the Chouans, as well as I, had judged this to be an important position; for, as we passed through these woods, we remarked that fortifications were begun. The *chateau* itself was in a fit state to maintain a siege, for all the window-shutters had embrasures.

Nevertheless, we approached without seeing anything that indicated an intention offering resistance, and we entered the house without firing a shot—but it was empty! It must have been evacuated by the garrison the moment the latter perceived the front of our columns, for we found a thousand rations of bread there. A calf recently slaughtered likewise attested that the inhabitants had not long quitted the *chateau*. Moreover, there was a great deal of linen for dressings and bandages, also a stock of ready prepared lint Lastly, we found more than fifty printed notices, fixing the night of the 3rd to the 4th of June for a general attack.

I returned to Nantes, where I found General Solignac very easy with regard to the movement indicated in the letters we had seized. He fancied that the seizure of their correspondence, and their being consequently aware that we were acquainted with their plans of battle, would prevent the Chouans from making any attempt on the day fixed. In vain did I try to abate his confidence, by representing to him the fresh evidence I had acquired of a speedy insurrection: nothing could convince him, and I therefore gave, without consulting him, such orders as I deemed necessary. They were addressed to all our military commanders, and directed them to be upon their guard.[4]

At this period I received from the war minister the answer to General Mocquery's report. It was as follows:—

Paris, May 27, 1832,
General, One o'clock in the afternoon.
I have this instant received your letter of the 25th of May, enclosing General Mocquery's report of the 24th, at five o'clock in the morning; likewise those from Machecoul and Clisson, relative to the meeting which took place at Amaillout, and the resolution come to by the rebels, to assemble their forces and attempt a *coup-de-main* upon Machecoul
I had already received intimation of these projects from the minister of the interior. I conclude that you have reported the meeting at Amaillout to General Solignac, as well as the plans of the rebels; and that you have, in concert with him, taken the necessary measures to repress the announced

---

4. Appendix, Nos. 7, 8, 9 and 10.

movement, and make the authors of, and participators in, these criminal attempts severely repent. I rely upon General Solignac having ordered the junction of such detachments as are feeble enough to be exposed to the attacks of the bands that have been reinforced, and that he has further directed the concentration of the troops upon the principal points.

Lastly, I presume that he has taken measures for making the National Guard assist in your operations, and has concerted to this effect with the administrative authorities.

I am persuaded that, until the return of General Solignac, you will neglect nothing to be in a state of preparation against every event.

Duke of Dalmatia,
Minister, Secretary of State.

I had already taken the measures to which the minister alluded, and I patiently awaited the event.

CHAPTER 9

Under Attack

On the 4th of June, at daybreak, General Solignac entered my room.

"Do you know what is passing?" he inquired.

"No. What is the matter?"

"The peasants of Louroux, Vallet, and Vertou are coming in from all quarters, and state that the tocsin is sounding."

" Oh! Oh!" I exclaimed.

"You take the news very quietly, general," said M. Solignac.

"No doubt I do."

"But the Chouans are assembling."

"Well! they will be dispersed."

"But you must give orders to that effect."

"Orders are already given."

"What, beforehand."

"Yes. Did I not warn you of this insurrection? Well, I have taken my measures accordingly. The Chouans are assembling at Vallet you say; now I can tell you that at Vallet there is a certain Citizen Georges; he is *chef-de-bataillon* in the 29th, and commandant of the district of Clisson, and I assure you he will cut out work for them. I can answer that their business will soon be done, for they have a good hand to deal with."

"Will there be men enough?"

"Yes, General; for I have taken care to centralize my troops. Those under the command of the *chef-de-bataillon* Georges are in cantonments precisely at Louroux, and Vallet. They have orders to advance straight to the meeting, however numerous it may be, attack it desperately, and defend themselves in the same manner, falling back, only at the last extremity, upon the headquarters of the district."

These dispositions tranquillized General Solignac a little, and we proceeded together to the Prefecture.

The news of the insurrection spread rapidly. Several *maires* of communes in the neighbourhood of Clisson had met at that place, and all agreed that it was the intention of the whole of the Chouans to assemble on that day. I therefore thought it urgent to send reinforcements to my brave friend Georges, and I accordingly ordered Colonel Duvivier to march upon Chapelle-Hulin, and observe Louroux and Vallet, whilst I proceeded to Aigrefeuille, whence I should be ready to support Vertou and Clisson.

The *maire* offered to accompany me, and I accepted the offer; but General Solignac would not consent to the movement, except on my giving him my word that I would return to Nantes the following day. It was eight o'clock before all these arrangements were terminated.

I immediately set out with two companies of picked men, and fifty moveable *gendarmes*. Two leagues before we reached Aigrefeuille, our scouts thought they perceived a movement to the left of the road; but, the country being covered with wood, it was impossible to quit the high-road, and I ordered the march to be continued. About a quarter of an hour after, we perceived smoke rising above the Maine, and the report of musketry reached us.

As the wind blew from us, it was difficult to judge of the importance of the action. I threw out my scouts on the side of the firing, and sent forward some troops to support them. In the mean time, I reached the post to which I was going, situated between Nantes and Aigrefeuille and not far from the latter. All the inhabitants were in great alarm. They informed me that ever since ten o'clock in the morning there was fighting going on at Maisdon and Chateau Thébaut, and it appeared that a body of Chouans from Montbert, were then in full march upon Aigrefeuille. I immediately set out for this place, leaving platoons at all the branches of the road to watch the motions of the enemy, and I arrived there just as the national guard was preparing to give the Chouans a warm reception.

Having encouraged it in these good intentions, I hastened to the scene of action, to which I was guided by the report of musketry, although it was beginning to subside. I obtained the particulars of the action from an officer whom I met, commanding a platoon of grenadier-*tirailleurs*. He informed me that the enemy, having been driven from Maisdon where they had taken up a strong position, had begun to retreat before our soldiers. I ordered Captain Teissier, with a company of *voltigeurs* of the 32nd, to support the pursuit. This detachment went energetically to work, overtook the band of Chouans at the ferry near Chateau-Thébaut, and killed several of them.

Meanwhile, I received intelligence that a considerable body of the retreating rebels had crossed the Maine, and fallen back upon Montbert, where the Chouans were assembled in considerable numbers. They were commanded by La Roberie, under the orders of Charrette and the Duchess of Berri. This made me regret having despatched my company of *voltigeurs*, which did not return till eight at night, and the men were so exhausted by fatigue that it was impossible to require further duty from them until they had taken rest. I therefore rallied my little body of troops, and returned with it to Aigrefeuille, where we were joined by the picked companies of the 29th. Here I learned the following particulars.

The *Chef-de-Bataillon* Georges, on receiving intelligence that an assembly of Chouans was forming at Maisdon, immediately ordered two picked companies, consisting in all of a hundred and twenty-nine men, to fall upon the rebels and disperse them. This injunction was most strictly obeyed. Twenty-five *voltigeurs* forming the vanguard, received, close to the very muzzle, the fire from the hedge; having returned it, they immediately charged bayonets, crossed the hedge and fell upon their assailants, who, having retired behind a second hedge, fired again. The report of the musketry brought up the remainder of our forces to the scene of action.

They advanced in doublequick time, and the Chouans, though eight hundred strong, were completely routed in two hours. The standing corn being however very high, the boldest of the rebels returned every now and then, stole within shot, and, by firing a shot or two, still kept up the action in a slight degree. I arrived whilst this was going on, and set upon the enemy with the fresh soldiers who accompanied me. This soon forced the rebels to retreat

They lost in this skirmish about a dozen in wounded. Charrette's *aide-de-camp* who had come to him with orders, was dangerously wounded, and his horse killed under him. On our side, we had only a serjeant-major of grenadiers belonging to the 29th, wounded; and this was extraordinary, for the Carlists had selected their field of battle extremely well. The platform of Maisdon is situated between the Maine and the Sévre, two deeply imbedded rivers, which consequently offer great means of defence. It was there, moreover, that the Chouans of Nantes, Clisson, Légé, Machecoul, Vallet, and Louroux, had orders to assemble, and it has since been clearly proved to us that if I had only left them till next day to carry their project into execution, their number would have amounted to eight thousand.

As soon as the action was over, I reported what had passed to General Solignac, stating all the particulars which I have here given. At nine o'clock in the evening of the same day, the fourth battalion of the National Guard of Nantes arrived. It was headed by a veteran of the army of Egypt, and commanded by Lieutenant-Colonel Paris, chief of the staff. During the march of this battalion, its scouts had made three prisoners: M. de Kersabiec, his servant, and a certain M. D——, all three well armed. It brought me likewise orders to attack Montbert.

This was a thing very easily talked about at Nantes, but extremely difficult to effect at Aigrefeuille. The battalion sent to me was too much fatigued for me to lead it into action before it had obtained some rest; and the troops with me, which would have answered my purpose perfectly well, if the pursued and dispersed Chouans had not had time to rally and renew the conflict, were no longer sufficiently numerous now that an unmolested rest of sixteen hours had allowed the rebels to assemble, and occupy the woods which defended the approach to Montbert. I was therefore obliged to defer the attack till the morrow.

At one o'clock in the morning I made my men fall in. My force consisted of four picked companies of infantry of the line, the fourth battalion of the National Guard of Nantes, and fifty mounted *gendarmes*—in all, seven hundred men. For the defence of Aigre-feuille, I left forty men from the centre companies of the 29th, together with a part of the National Guard of the place. Having formed my little army into two columns, I placed myself at the head of the battalion of the National Guard of Nantes, two of the picked companies, and my fifty horsemen. I gave the command of the other column to Lieutenant-Colonel Paris, with orders to turn the castle of Montbert, and attack it from the opposite side. This castle, being situated upon a height, is capable of being well defended.

As the road I had taken was the most direct, I reached Montbert the first. We entered it at four o'clock in the morning, but found no other signs of rebellion there, than a white flag waving over the church-tower. This sight exasperated the national guards, and I took advantage of this feeling to lead them immediately to the attack of the castle, which we forced.

Although the peasants, either from fear or from an unwillingness to second our intentions, did not reply to our questions concerning the direction which La Roberie had taken with his forces, I should not the less have pursued, and most probably have overtaken him, had I not received the night before an order from General Solignac to be at Nantes on the evening of the 5th. I had just heard that the Duchess of Berri and Charrette had been at Montbert, and that circumstance increased my regret; but I was forced to obey the orders of my commanding officer, and with great reluctance, I gave directions for our departure.

Having received no intelligence from my cantonment at St. Philibert, I directed the two picked companies of the 29th to separate from us, in order to effect a communication with this cantonment, whilst I marched direct to Nantes with the other two picked companies, the battalion of the national guard, and my escort of *gendarmes.*

I had already, with the front of my column, passed Les Sorinières, which is the last stage before you reach Nantes, when I was overtaken by an express, who brought me intelligence that La Roberie had returned and taken up a position at Pont-James. I could not at first credit this; but, being at length convinced that it was true, I left my two companies at Les Sorinières and entered Nantes, fully persuaded that General Solignac would consent to the request I intended to make him, to be allowed immediately to return and attack La Roberie.

He however refused, without giving me any reasonable motive for doing so; and I have never been able to comprehend this refusal. It was a serious error; for I should have arrived in time to have taken a share in the action at Vieillevigne, and should, probably, have made both Charrette and the Duchess of Berri prisoners. In consequence of General Solignac's determination I was induced to write to him as follows:

General,

I had the honour to report to you the particulars of my expedition, yesterday, to the environs of Aigrefeuille, Montbert, and Maisdon. But as I passed through Les Sorinières on my way back, I was informed that La Roberie had returned to Pout-James at the head of a tolerably numerous body. Judging that he was in a position favourable for attack, I provisionally left two picked companies at Les Sorinières, in the full persuasion that the plan I was about to submit to you would meet with your approbation.

I have given orders to the detachments at Légé, St Philibert, Machecoul, and Aigrefeuille, to march upon Pont-James. I will take a hundred infantry and fifty *gendarmes*, and will immediately set out at their head for Pont-James by the road to Sables. With such dispositions, it is impossible that La Roberie can escape. Yield to my entreaties, I earnestly beg of you in the name of the public interest, and I assure you that I will give you a good account of La Roberie, and all those by whom he is accompanied. I have, moreover, considered it my duty to make you this proposal in order to secure my responsibility from any imputations hereafter.

I was upon thorns; the sound of musketry was thundering in my ears; I had not slept for seventy-two hours,—and yet, the whole night after this strange refusal by General Solignac, I could not close my eyes.

This resolution taken by the commander-in-chief was not applicable to me alone: it extended at the same time to Colonel Duvivier; and, as this officer had returned from Vallet with the troops under his command, all the country was now free, and the Chouans had full liberty again to assemble unmolested. When I reached Nantes, Colonel Duvivier had already set out on his return to Ancenis, where he was to oppose the attempt of La Roche Macé [1]

On the morning of the 6th, I again renewed my application to General Solignac without any better success. I felt instinctively, however, that some fighting must have occurred; and indeed we received news, the same evening, that an encounter had taken place at Vieillevigne, at which the Duchess of Berri was present. She had dressed the wounds of the men with her own hands, and had escaped only by changing horses with Charrette, who with great difficulty avoided being taken prisoner.

Another action took place on the same day, much more destructive, and the particulars of which are also much more interesting.

A meeting of Chouans had been appointed for the 6th, at the *chateau* of La Penissière de la Cour, situated a league and a half from Clisson. The object of this meeting was to march against Cugnau and La Buffière, and disarm the national guard. At nine o'clock in the morning, forty-five Chouans were assembled at the place appointed. They were all young men of family, and were commanded by two brothers, ex-officers in the royal guard. They had with them two peasants, who, having learnt at Nantes to play upon the light-infantry bugle, constituted their band of military music.

---

1. See M. de Coislin's letter to this Vendean chief (Chapter 6).

The adjutant-major of the 29th being informed in the absence of the *chef-de-bataillon* Georges, that this meeting was to take place, put himself at the head of forty-five *voltigeurs* and two *gendarmes*, and proceeded to the *chateau* of La Penissière de la Cour. On reaching it, he found that his detachment was not sufficiently numerous to invest the habitation, which was defended by a wall forming the enclosure of a park. A *gendarme* was therefore despatched for reinforcements, and ninety men arrived, who were soon after followed by forty more under the command of Lieutenant Saneo. The adjutant-major now ordered an attack to be made. After a short defence an external wall was abandoned, and the Chouans retreated into the house, where they barricaded all the doors.

They then stationed their forces in the ground-floor and the first floor, placing on either floor a peasant with his bugle, who did not cease playing during the whole action; and from the windows they opened a fire, which was well sustained and very ably directed. Twice did the soldiers advance within twenty yards of the house, and as often were they repulsed.

The adjutant-major ordered a third attack, and, whilst preparations were making for it, four men, aided by a mason, advanced towards the *chateau*, selecting as their point of advance, part of the gable-end which had no opening into the garden, and the approach to which could not therefore be defended. Having reached the wall in safety, they placed a ladder against it, and, ascending to the roof of the house, made an opening, threw lighted combustibles into the garrets, and then withdrew. In an instant, a column of smoke burst from the roof, through which the fire soon made its way.

The soldiers now uttered loud shouts of triumph, and again marched towards the little citadel, which seemed to have a standard of flame planted upon its summit. The besieged had perceived the fire, but had not time to extinguish it; and, as fire has always a tendency to ascend, they hoped that when the roof was destroyed, it would be naturally extinguished for want of something to feed it. They therefore replied to the shouts of our soldiers with a volley of musketry, as well sustained as the former; and, during the whole time it lasted, the bugles continued playing warlike flourishes.

At this juncture, the *chef-de-bataillon* Georges arrived with a few more men. He immediately ordered the charge to be beat, and the men, in emulation of each other, rushed towards the *chateau*.

This time they reached the doors of the building, and the sappers and miners prepared to break them open. The officers commanding the Chouans, directed those stationed on the ground-floor to ascend to the story above it. This order was immediately obeyed; and, whilst the sappers were breaking open the doors, half of the besieged continued to fire at their assailants, whilst the other half occupied themselves in taking up the paving-tiles and making holes through the floor, so that the moment the soldiers entered, they were received with a volley muzzle-to, fired through the intervals between the beams and rafters.

The assailants were forced to retreat, and the Chouans hailed this event with their screeching bugles and loud cries of "Long live Henry V!"

The *chef-de-bataillon* now directed that the ground-floor should be set on fire in the same manner as the garrets had been. Accordingly, the men advanced with lighted torches and dry wood, all of which they threw into the house through the windows, and in ten minutes the Chouans had fire at their feet as well as over their heads. It seemed therefore impossible for them to escape death; and the firing which they kept up, and which had not intermitted for a single moment, appeared to be the last act of vengeance of resolute men driven to desperation.

And in truth their situation was dreadful.

The fire soon reached the beams, and the rooms were filled with smoke, which escaped through the windows. The garrison had therefore nothing left but the choice of three modes of quitting life: to be burned to death, suffocated by smoke, or massacred by our soldiers.

The commanders of the rebels adopted a desperate course: they resolved to make a sortie. But, to give it the least chance of success, it was necessary that it should be protected by a fire of musketry which would occupy the attention of our soldiers; they therefore asked who among them would volunteer to sacrifice themselves for the safety of their comrades. Eight offered their services.

The little band was therefore divided into two platoons. Thirty-five men and a bugle-player were to make an attempt to reach the other extremity of the park, enclosed only with a hedge; and the eight others, with the remaining bugle-player, were to protect the attempt. The two brothers embraced each other, for they were to separate: one commanded the garrison that remained, the other led the sortie.

In consequence of these arrangements, and whilst those who remained continued, by running from window to window, to keep up a tolerably brisk fire, the others made a hole in the wall opposite to the side attacked; and on a passage sufficiently large being opened they came forth in good order, the bugle at their head, marching in double-quick time towards the extremity of the park where the hedge was.

Their retreat brought upon them a discharge of musketry which killed two. A third, being mortally wounded, expired near the hedge. The bugle-player at the head of the little band received three balk in his body, and still continued to play. It is a pity that I dare not publish the names of such men.

Meanwhile, the situation of the eight men who remained in the house had become more and more dangerous. The burning rafters cracked and seemed no longer able to bear the weight of the besieged, who therefore retired into a species of recess formed by the wall, resolved to defend themselves there to the last extremity; and they had scarcely reached it when the floor fell in with a dreadful crash. The soldiers uttered shouts of joy at this event; for the musketry ceased to annoy them at the same instant, and they thought the garrison had been crushed in the ruins. This error saved the lives of the eight heroic Vendeans.

When the Chouans, from their recess, perceived that the besiegers were convinced they had fallen into the immense furnace which blazed fearfully below them, they remained silent and motionless. Our soldiers, on the other hand, with a horror quite natural in such a case, speedily quitted a burning building whose flames devoured at the same time both friends and enemies, whether alive or dead. Meanwhile, night soon came, and amid its darkness the eight men supposed to have been either crushed to death or burned alive, glided like wandering spectres along the heated walls, and reached in safety the hedge through which their companions had escaped; so that there remained nothing upon the field of battle except the red and smoking house, and around it a few corpses rendered visible by the last flashes of the expiring flame.[2]

---

2. See in Appendix, No. 11. the report of the *chef-de-bataillon* Georges.

CHAPTER 10

Duchess Escapes

On the evening of the 7th, I at length obtained leave from General Solignac to pursue the plan I had recommended to him so many days previously, and I lost not a moment in taking advantage of it to commence my expedition forthwith.

As I crossed the bridge of Pyrmile, I asked the officer on duty there, whether the Clisson diligence was come yet, as a delay of two hours in its arrival had already occurred, and this was a source of great uneasiness to me. He replied in the affirmative, but stated that both the conductor and the passengers had informed him that there was fighting going on at La Penissière de la Cour, where a body of Chouans were besieged by the troops of the line and the national guard.

I had no uneasiness about Clisson, because I knew the commandant Georges to be there; I therefore took the road to Machecoul, which, being unprotected by troops, gave me greater ground for apprehension.

At two o'clock in the morning, and in spite of a heavy, beating rain, I reached Port-Saint-Père, always accompanied by my two faithful picked companies, the soldiers of which must really have had limbs of iron to follow me as they did. We there found eight hundred men belonging to the national guard of the district of Paimboeuf.

As we passed, we searched the *chateau* of M. Aristide Grainville, in which we supposed the Duchess of Berri might have been concealed, but found nothing there.

After this operation, we continued our march, and arrived at

Machecoul about nine o'clock in the morning. All was perfectly quiet at that place, and I was informed that such of the inhabitants as had been compelled to leave their work and join the Chouans would gladly have returned to their homes; the fear of punishment alone keeping them in the ranks of the rebels. I immediately issued the following proclamation, which I ordered to be distributed through the country, and which produced the best possible effect.

Inhabitants of the Country.

Four days only have now elapsed since, having placed confidence in the promises of the nobles who are the enemies of our liberties, you first raised the standard of rebellion, and already have several of the chiefs who promised you victory received the reward of their base treachery. The prisons of Nantes are glutted, and by those missing from among you, you may ascertain the number of your leaders who have become victims to their own blind folly.

Ye young men, who think ye will escape from the conscription by enlisting under the banner of these noble egotists, what have ye gained by following them? Defeat, and the shame of being forced, as Frenchmen, to fly from your own countrymen; for wherever you have assembled, there also have you been dispersed. Do you not tremble lest your crops, so plentiful in appearance, should be destroyed by the scourge of civil war? What can you obtain in exchange for fighting?

And what do you expect from the promises of all those nobles who only make use of you for the promotion of their personal interests, and who, the moment you become of no farther use to them, will attempt to replunge you into servitude, and take from you the little property you have acquired since the revolution? Young men, are you not all of you Frenchmen? Are you not our brethren? and think you that, when necessity forces us to fight against you, our hearts do not bleed at the wounds we inflict upon you?

Come back to us! We will open our arms to receive you. Return to your homes, deliver up your arms at the munici-

palities, and do not fear the least resentment from us. All shall be forgotten, and your return shall expiate your fault."
Machecoul, June 7th, 1832.

After this, I took measures for making the roost effective search throughout the country, and for this object I organized two moveable columns, composed half of national guards and half of troops of the line. Having explained to one the district it would have to explore, I proceeded with the other to the *chateau* of La Chalotière, a vast and ancient manor-house, surrounded by a magnificent park, and which, from its lone situation, was said to serve the Chouans as a place of retreat The search I made there was unattended, however, with any result

I immediately after pushed on to St. Etienne de Mer-Morte, where I found no other traces of the Chouans than two freshly covered graves in the churchyard. Two Vendeans, killed on the 5th at La Caraterie, a *chateau* belonging to M. de Cornullier, lay buried there.

On returning from this place I went to Paulx, a somewhat considerable burgh, whose name stands in the central register as supplying six hundred men. I here halted to refresh my column, and proceeded to the only inn in the place. No sooner was I seated there than an orderly came to inform me that a gentleman without his coat, and in a fine white shirt, was in the stable-yard cleaning three horses. I immediately directed that he should be brought before me; and five minutes after he entered the room in which I was sitting.

On asking his name and profession, he replied by showing me his passport, and his commission as postmaster for supplying post-horses, at a place near Toulouse. He came to La Vendée, he said, for the purpose of purchasing horses at the fair of St. Gervais. In fact, this fair was to begin next day, and we were only four leagues from the village in which it was held.

Nevertheless, as the account he gave of himself did not appear to me quite satisfactory, I ordered him to be searched by my *gendarmes*. Like all the Carlists, he wore a scapulary suspended from his neck; to this scapulary was attached a gold heart surmounted by a small cross, on which was engraven, "God and the King." He wore, moreover, a belt containing five thousand *francs* in gold, for which I gave him a receipt; and, having drawn up a *procès-verbal*,, I delivered him in charge to the *gendarmes*, who almost immediately after brought me a brace of horse-pistols and a long Italian *stiletto*, which they had found in the holsters of his saddle.

There could be no further doubt that this prisoner belonged to the Carlist army. I was afterwards informed that one of the horses upon which, when discovered, he was performing the office of groom, had been ridden by the Duchess of Berri. From this circumstance, my soldiers called him nothing but "the Duchess."

This was the only capture I made. The Duchess escaped and remained at Pauls, concealed in the cottage of a peasant.

I now turned my attention towards reestablishing the *maire* of Paulx in his office, airing found him at Machecoul, whither he had fled during the danger. I escorted this functionary to his house; and, in order to give greater solemnity to his re-installation, I pardoned forty Chouans whom he presented to me as belonging to his commune. I made them a military harangue, at the conclusion of which I told them that I placed the *maire* entirely under their safeguard. They annexed for his safety, and kept their word; for I afterwards ascertained that nothing further had occurred to trouble his security.

I further ordered them to deliver up their arms, and sign their submission in the registers of the commune. This they immediately complied with. Their example was followed by all the Chouans who dwelt in the neighbouring villages, against whom, from that period, no further proceedings, were carried on. By such means, the whole district was pacified in the course of a few days.

The ceremony of the *maire's* re-installation being over, I resumed my march, directing my detachment upon the village of La Marne, where I had ordered the Commandant Philippeau to meet me. I found him just returning from Sainte-Luminé-de-Cousait, where, he had made a *battue,* as well as in its environs, without finding any traces of the Chouans, although on the previous day it had been invested by more than eight hundred rebels. The only capture he had made was a young man wounded in the leg, who stated that he had received his wound at the combat of Vieillevigne. It was he who informed us that the Duchess of Berri had been present at this action, and had dressed the men's wounds. I returned to Machecoul the same evening, after having made my detachment cover, in the course of the day, more than twelve leagues of ground.[1] This did not prevent me from ordering, for the next day (9th), a fresh *battue* in the marsh of Bouaine.

We accordingly started at two o'clock in the morning, and having divided my troops into two columns, we reached Bouaine by two opposite roads. Here, however, we found everything, perfectly quiet, and we therefore resumed our march to return to Machecoul, which we reached after as hard a day's work as the preceding.

I here found a letter from General Solignac, ordering me to return the next day to Nantes, with the men under my command.

The remainder of the day I employed in reviewing the national guard, and I informed the men composing it that they might return to their homes on the morrow. They were animated by the best feelings, and regretted only that they had not discovered a body of Chouans which they might have fallen upon. We parted the best friends in the world.

On Sunday morning the 10th of June I set out for Nantes, with my prisoner, whom I wished to keep near my person. Lest any misfortune should befall him, I sent all my *gendarmes*, with the exception of three, on an expedition to the marsh. The three I had retained composed my sole escort; for my infantry columns did not march fast enough. Having set off at a hand-gallop, I left the infantry behind me. I had thus to cross four leagues of country in a state of insurrection, which, strictly speaking, was not very prudent; but I felt a full confidence that, after forty years of warfare with grape-shot, I should not at last be killed by a contemptible ball from behind a hedge.

And indeed, I reached Port-Saint-Père in safety. Immediately

---

1. About twenty-eight miles.—Tr.

on my arrival, I proceeded with my captured Chouan to the residence of the *maire*. I here found the family at breakfast, and, on being invited to partake of the meal, I required no pressing to accept the offer, only I requested the master of the house to extend his kind invitation to my secretary,—pointing to M. de Puylaroc, my prisoner. This, as it may well be imagined, was complied with in the politest manner, and my sham secretary also took his place at the breakfast-table.

Nevertheless, however hungry he might have been, he by no means felt at ease. The conversation was entirely on the subject of the Chouans, and it was asked, by what sort of magic the civil war, expected to have been long and sanguinary, had suddenly ceased? All the honours of this pacification were attributed to me, and each praise was followed by a toast of success to me, and death to the Chouans. At each toast my poor secretary made a wry face. This was fortunately attributed to the tartness of the wine, which was the production of the host's own vineyard.

From generalities the company soon proceeded to particulars; and I was asked to relate the circumstance of the arrest of the gentleman in the fine shirt, who was found acting the part of a groom towards three horses in the court-yard of the inn at Paulx. I referred the question to my secretary, who, as I informed him, was better acquainted with the particulars than I was. He related the whole affair with a tolerably good grace; but one of the company having asked him why I had not ordered the rascal to be shot, he referred the inquirer to me. All the reasons for clemency which I could urge, seemed to have but little weight, for the party rose from the table in the midst of a general chorus, declaring that the prisoner ought to have been put to death immediately.

I thought this unanimity of feeling not very gratifying to my poor devil of a secretary; therefore, having perceived the front of my first column of infantry entering the village, I seized this as a pretext for taking leave of these enthusiasts, and went out to meet my troops. I directed Captain Teissier, who commanded the column, to make a halt at Port-Saint-Père, rest the men, and not return to Nantes till next day; for I had made the poor fellows under his command perform on an average fifteen leagues a day, ever since they had been out.

Having still five leagues to travel before I reached Nantes, I set out immediately after I had given these orders. On reaching the suburbs of the city, a woman called out, "Oh! here comes the General with another Chouan!"

This convinced me that my prisoner had been recognised, and that it would be difficult to save his life if I did not hasten forward. I therefore dismissed two of my escort, and, having directed the remaining *gendarme* to follow me, and M. de Puylaroc to follow him, we trotted on. In this manner we proceeded through the city without any further attention being paid to the prisoner, whom I brought in safety to my own house.

The moment I got off my horse, I proceeded to the residence of General Solignac, and reported to him the particulars of my expedition.

On the 12th, I set out for Chateaubriand, but had no sooner reached that place, than) received intelligence of the return of General Bonnet to Nantes. He had come to resume the chief command of the Fourth, Twelfth, and Thirteenth military divisions. Few things could have proved more agreeable to me than this information; it induced me to set out immediately for Nantes, where I arrived about eight o'clock in the evening. I had thus ridden fifteen leagues in five hours and a half; and yet I arrived in time to pay my respects to the new general-in-chief on the same evening.

The very next day, his presence at Nantes was easily perceived: the movements had resumed their activity and simultaneousness, whilst, prior to that time, the negligence in this respect had been so great, that even up to the 15th of June, the placing of the city in a state of siege had not yet been officially made known to the *maire*. I took General Bonnet's orders on the subject: he directed me to go through these necessary forms; and, having done so, I returned next day to Chateaubriand for the purpose of terminating the operations which I had there begun.

When I came back to Nantes, I urged the prefect to issue a

proclamation to the people over whom he exercised jurisdiction, stating that the placing of the city in a state of siege need not prevent the civil and military authorities from acting together in concert. I likewise pressed him to collect all arrears of taxes. In the mean time, the octave of Corpus-Christi having arrived, I ordered all the military commandants to protect the religious ceremonies of this festival, in order to deprive the priests of the least pretence for complaining, which they would not have failed to do without this precaution.

I was at Savenai when I heard that the trial of M. de Kersabiec, and the sentence passed upon that individual by the first court-martial, were likely to cause some disturbance; I therefore started *en poste,* at ten o'clock at night, accompanied by my *aide-decamp*, and arrived at Nantes in time to witness the riots, in which General Solignac adopted a line of conduct that occasioned his recall.

I shall not here dwell upon the disputes which took place between the two generals; the whole affair has been published, and everyone has been able to make up his mind as to which of them was to blame, and which in the right. All I can say is this: I would not for the world have to begin again the fortnight I spent, constantly pressed between the contending self-loves of these two gentlemen. At length the appointment of General Count d'Erlon to the chief command of the division, put an end to these conflicts, and enabled me to resume my excursions.

My first expedition was for the purpose of establishing a garrison of eighty *voltigeurs* in the *chateau* belonging to the Marquis de Coislin—having obtained authority to do so. This measure was one of very great importance, because M. de Coislin had made the peasants believe he was so powerful that the government would never dare to attack him personally. I however gave strict orders that this beautiful estate should be respected, and Madame de Coislin's certificate [2] is a proof that my instructions were attended to.

About this time, I had a search made at the *chateau* of La Violey, belonging to General Clouet, where several letters and a singular brevet were found. I here give one of the letters, because it

2. See Appendix, No. 12.

seems to me to contain a great deal of wit, and the brevet, because it appears a curious document. The letter shows how little the ministers were justified in talking of a pretended Carlo-republican alliance; nevertheless, I shall not state who the writer is, though, in good truth, it would not be unfair to name her. Many worse things have been written without the authors having even thought of remaining unknown.

June 18th, 1831.

Your young friend, my dear General,

cannot repress the desire he feels to embrace you, in order worthily to celebrate the anniversary of that delightful campaign at Algiers. The other day we drank to the health of our brave men of those good days; and I hope you will have perceived it, by an increase of the vigour of life. During this time, General Dumoustier was dying, from the recent amputation of one of his legs, which in these latter times he had made use of badly enough for him to believe in its being a punishment inflicted by God; for it was a fall in one of his fine excursions against us that occasioned all his sufferings and this his last misfortune. He was a protestant, as you know, so that our clergy have nothing whatever to do with his carcass, in honour of which all the artillery of Nantes has been fired. This must not, however, be made a subject of reproach to him, for it is the last noise the poor devil will ever make in this world. It is thus that all goes off in smoke; and it is truly worthwhile to do so much harm! We may, however, be made to regret him, by having a worse sent to us. [3]

You see by the public journals how the republic is in preparation. Its principles reach even the army; what has occurred in the south is a proof of this. There is a regiment now passing through this place on its march to Brittany, the officers of which boast loudly of their republican principles. We shall, I trust, be separated into two very distinct camps,

---

3. General Solignac was appointed to succeed him.

which will be much better. All those men of the *juste-milieu* do nothing but dirt and begrime everything they touch; they are more embarrassed than ever, here, to prevent the stupid fricassee from turning, which they have made with such heterogeneous ingredients. In vain do they shake the stew-pan, nothing will mix, and the whole compound will some day or other not very far distant, fly out and scald their faces.

The speedy planting of a tree of liberty at Nantes is announced to us. You are aware of the scandalous occurrence during the procession at Sainte-Croix. Cavaignac had gone to Nantes for the purpose of exciting the public feelings, and he departed in a great rage at not finding more than fifty men of energy in that city; and, in fact, there are not more than two or three hundred rogues in the whole city of Nantes capable of showing energy *à la* Cavaignac. But when they are all in motion, they think themselves innumerable. No prisoner arrives, but they want to eat him alive. It makes one shudder. They would fain revive all the horrors of 1793.[4]

I always entertain the hope that everything will end well. I know not why I have such a hope, but the fact is, I have it. I have it not in the same manner as all those others: I do not depend upon success by arms—I do not depend upon human will—I do not depend, in fine, upon such means as are generally employed;—and yet I have hope. I often accuse myself of folly—and yet I have hope. I see, I hear, I learn everything that tends the most to excite despair, impatience, and discouragement;—and still I have hope. I tell you, I do not understand my own feelings, but I believe that constancy alone, combined with patient firmness, is the strongest of our means.

That Poland still lives, I admire it in spite of myself, for I love the Emperor Nicholas; but the Poles are certainly a brave people, and ought to despise our revolutionists. Such an

---

4. I hope M. Cavaignac will be the first to laugh at this Carlist sally; and above all, that he will be persuaded of the esteem I entertain for his character.

alliance is unworthy of them; they are only pot-house ac-
quaintances. I think the Russians will have work enough there
to last them the whole year.

Have you any good news from your wife and your dear
children? Olivier will give me all the particulars on his
return. Our young man is firm, and he would be thought a
complete savage by those elegant Parisians, whom I detest
more and more. We appear to them mad, and nothing else.
In their judgment, wisdom lies in infamy, and they mistake
indignation for brain-fever. Their theatres are filled with obscen-
ity and impiety, and they laugh at everything. Good God!

I leave on the 30th, that is to say, next Thursday week. If,
however, between this and that we should have a republic,
I think I should remain here. There are still twelve days to run
before that period arrives, and twelve days in these times may
bring many changes. Oh! the delightful age we live in!
Adieu.[5]

Next comes the brevet:

Brother Antoine, Abbot of our lady of La Trappe de Mill-
eray, of the strict observance of the order of Cistercians in
the Diocess of Nantes, to Monsieur Anne-Louis-Antoine
Clouet, Knight of St. Louis, and officer of the Legion of
Honour.

Health in Christ Jesus our Lord.

Although the laws of Christian charity oblige us to pray to
God for all men in general, we nevertheless consider ourselves more strictly obliged to pray for those persons who
express a wish that we should do so, and place some confidence in our prayers. Therefore, sir, we, being informed
that you entertain such feelings towards us, do willingly
grant you these our letters of association which you have
demanded of us, trusting in the infinite mercy of God, on

---

5. Though General Dermoncourt has not thought proper to give the name of the
fair writer of this letter, we, who have not the same scruples, here insert it. The letter
was written by the Marchioness de Coislin.

the powerful intercession of the blessed Virgin Mary, our patroness, and on that of our devout father St. Bernard and the other saints protectors of our order. Notwithstanding our sense of our own unworthiness, we promise you that, during the whole course of our lives, you shall share in all our acts of piety, religion, and penitence; in the communion of our brethren; even in the holy sacrifices at our altars; and generally in all doing and henceforward to be done in this monastery, by the operation of the spirit of God; and lastly, when we receive news of your death, we will take care to implore the Lord to grant you a full and entire remission of your sins, and to put you in possession of the repose of his saints.

Moreover, we trust, sir, that this engagement will be reciprocal: that is to say, that you will make us participators in the merit of your good works, and remember us in your prayers. This, in the strongest manner, we conjure you to do.

Made at our monastery this 22nd day of July, 1821.

B. Antoine,

Abbot, though unworthy

B. Vincent, Prior.

B. Jules.

B. Thomas.

B. Etienne.

By command of the Reverend Father Abbot,

B. Alexis, Secretary.

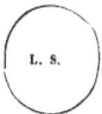

This represents the seal of the monastery, bearing an imprint of the Virgin Mary.

CHAPTER 11

Travelling Incognito

Meanwhile, my moveable columns continued their movements on the other side of the Loire, and hunted down the Chouans wherever they appeared. The Duchess of Berri, who would not leave the kingdom, notwithstanding the earnest entreaties made to induce her to do so, had always someone or other of my detachments at her heels. One day her harness was taken; it was recognised as belonging to her by a saddle of red velvet, embroidered with gold. At another time her wardrobe was captured, and she was obliged to continue her flight with nothing but the clothes she had on.

It may well be supposed that this kind of life was intolerable. Being thus pursued, the duchess had never an entire night of sleep; and, when daylight came, danger and fatigue awoke with her. A new plan was then adopted by the Vendean chiefs, and communicated to the duchess, who approved of it. She was to proceed to Nantes, where an asylum had long been prepared for her.

We should then lose all traces of her in the country, and, during the further searches which would necessarily follow her disappearance, and draw from Nantes the few troops stationed there, the Chouans were to enter the city on a market-day, disguised as peasants, get possession of the castle by a *coup-de-main*, and immediately place the duchess within its walls;—then declare Nantes the provisional capital of the kingdom, and proclaim the deposition of Louis-Philippe, together with the regency of the Duchess of

Berri. To facilitate the execution of this enterprise, Her Royal Highness was to reside as near to the castle as possible. For men in despair, this plan was not deficient either in boldness or in ability. It is true that, in all these combinations, the chiefs calculated greatly upon the presence of mind and courage of the duchess; and in this they were right:—for it was La Vendée which failed the duchess, not the duchess who failed La Vendée.

They deliberated some time on the safest mode of entering Nantes. The duchess closed the debate by stating, that she would enter it on foot, in the dress of a peasant-girl, accompanied only by Mademoiselle Eulalie de Kersabiec and M. de Ménars.

In consequence of this decision, the Duchess of Berri set out, on the very next market-day, which I believe was the 16th of June, at six o'clock in the morning, from a cottage at which she had slept, situated in the neighbourhood of Chateau-Thibaud. Mademoiselle de Kersabiec was dressed like the duchess, and M. de Ménars as a farmer. They had five leagues to journey on foot.

After travelling half an hour in this trim, the thick, nailed shoes and worsted stockings, to which the duchess was not accustomed, hurt her feet. Still she attempted to walk; but, judging that if she continued to wear these shoes and stockings, she should soon be unable to proceed, she seated herself upon the bank of a ditch, took them off, thrust them into her large pockets, and continued her journey barefoot.

A moment after, having remarked the peasant-girls who passed her on the road, she perceived that the fineness of her skin, and the aristocratic whiteness of her legs, were likely to betray her; she therefore went to the road-side, took some dark-coloured earth, and after rubbing her legs with it, resumed her walk. She had still four leagues to travel before she reached the place of her destination.

This sight, it must be confessed, was an admirable theme to draw philosophical reflections from those who accompanied her. They beheld a woman who, two years before, had her place of Queen-Mother at the Tuileries, and possessed Chambord and Bagatelle; rode out in a carriage drawn by six horses, with escorts of body-guards resplendent with gold and silver—who went to the representation of theatrical pieces acted expressly for her, preceded by runners shaking their torches—who filled the theatre with her sole presence, and, on her return to her palace, reached her splendid bed-chamber, walking upon double cushions from Persia and Turkey, lest the floor should gall her delicate little feet:—this woman, the only one of her family, perhaps, who had done nothing to deserve her misfortunes, they now saw, still covered with the smoke of the action at Vieillevigne, beset with danger, proscribed, a price set upon her head, and whose only escort and court consisted of an old man and a young girl,—going to seek an asylum from which she might perhaps be shut out, clad in the garments of a peasant, walking barefoot upon the angular sand and sharp pebbles of the road. And it was not she who suffered, hut her companions: they had tears in their eyes, and she, laughter, jests, and consolation in her mouth. Oh! these are curious times we live in, when almost every country has its kings who wander barefoot through the highways!

Meanwhile, the distance became progressively shorter, and, in proportion as they got nearer to Nantes, their fears subsided. The duchess had become accustomed to her attire, and the country-people on the road did not seem to perceive that the little peasant-woman who tripped lightly by them, was any other than her dress indicated. It was already a great point gained in deceive the instinct of penetration peculiar to the inhabitants of this country, and who are rivalled, if not surpassed in this quality, only by soldiers inured to warfare.

At length, Nantes appeared in sight, and the duchess put on her shoes and stockings to enter the town. On reaching the Pont Pyrmile, she found herself in the midst of a detachment commanded by an officer formerly in the royal guard, and whom she recognised as having often seen him on duty at her palace.

Opposite to the Bouffai, somebody tapped the duchess on the shoulder; she started and turned round. The person guilty of this familiarity was an old apple-woman, who had placed her basket of fruit on the ground and was unable by herself to replace it upon her head.

"My good girls," she said, addressing the duchess and Mademoiselle de Kersabiec, "help me, pray, to take up my basket, and I will give each of you an apple."

The Duchess of Berri immediately seized a handle of the basket, made a sign to her companion to take the other, and the load was quickly placed in equilibrium upon the head of the old woman, who was going away without giving the promised reward, when the duchess seized her by the arm, and said: "Stop, mother, where's my apple?"

The old woman having given it to her, she was eating it with an appetite sharpened by a walk of five leagues, when, raising her eyes, they fell upon a placard headed by these three words in very large letters:

STATE OF SIEGE

This was the Ministerial decree which outlawed four departments of La Vendée, and set a price upon the duchess's head. She approached the placard and calmly read it through, notwithstanding the remonstrances of Mademoiselle de Kersabiec, who pressed her to hasten to the house where she was expected. But the duchess replied that the placard concerned herself too nearly for her not to make herself acquainted with its contents. The alarm of her two companions, whilst she was reading it, may easily be imagined.

At length she resumed her walk, and in a few minutes reached the house at which she was expected. There she took off her clothes covered with dirt, which are now preserved there as relics. She soon afterwards proceeded to the residence of Mesdemoiselles Deguigny, Rue Haute-du-Chateau, No. 3, where an apartment was prepared for her, and, within this apartment, a place of concealment. The apartment was nothing but a *mansarde* on the third floor consisting of two small rooms; and the place of concealment was a recess within an angle closed by the chimney of the innermost room. An iron plate formed the entrance to the hiding-place, and was opened by a spring.

From a life of the greatest agitation, the duchess suddenly passed to a state of the most complete inactivity. Her correspondence, which she always wrote herself, served to kill a few hours during the day, but the others seemed to her of dreadful length. She employed them in manual labour very foreign to her habits, and to the habits of those whom she made to share it with her. For instance, with the assistance of M. de Ménars, she entirely pasted on the grey paper which covered the walls of her *mansarde*. Her most habitual occupation, however, was painting flowers and tapestry, in which she excels. On the least subject of alarm, a bell was rung, which reached from the ground-floor to her bedchamber and gave the signal for concealment within the recess.

The Duchess of Berri took her meals on the second floor. She admitted to her table M. de Ménars, Mademoiselle Stylite de Kersabiec, who had joined the party, the two Demoiselles Deguigny, and lastly, M. Guibourg, who after his escape from the prison of Nantes, also took refuge in the same house, three weeks before the duchess was apprehended. These meals were often interrupted by false alarms, caused by military detachments entering or leaving the town. In this manner the Duchess of Berri spent five months.

Meanwhile, the activity with which I pursued the Chouans left them no means of concerting with each other for the execution of the plan I have before mentioned. Moreover, the head and life of the party was no longer with them. The Fifty-Sixth regiment of the line, sent to me towards the end of June, gave me an opportunity of rendering my pursuit more rigorous, and giving greater activity to my measures. I accordingly reinforced my cantonments, and established moveable columns, which scoured the country in all directions; and the *partisans* of Henry V. soon lost all hope of kindling civil war to any dangerous extent.

For some time past, however, a report was in circulation that the Duchess of Berri was at Nantes. This report was a certainty to me: my agents had brought me positive proofs of her presence in that city, and I had reported the same to superior authority. But, as the place of her concealment was known only to very few persons, and these persons were entirely devoted to her, there were not many chances of discovering where she was, whatever degree of credit the civil and military authorities might have attached to my sources of information.

Moreover, in her new place of refuge, the duchess had become an object of special surveillance. A sort of *coterie* had possession of her person, and would allow no one to see her. Even M. Bourmont had great difficulty in obtaining an interview with her.

About this period, Deutz arrived at Paris.

I will forego the repugnance which a military man naturally feels to mention a being of this description, whom I should never pass in the street without bestowing a horsewhipping upon him, did I not think my horse would be degraded by being afterwards flogged with the same whip. Treachery has, however, become so common within the last ten years, that traitors are the historical men of our period.

But such periods always exist in the decline of every monarchy, and must needs have their chronicles as if they were days of victory, in order to leave no hiatus in the history of nations. I will therefore state all I know concerning Deutz, having received the information from the individuals with the duchess, as well as from herself. As for this execrable monster himself, I never beheld him.

Hyacinth Simon Deutz was born at Cologne in 1802. When eighteen or twenty years of age he became a journeyman printer at M. Didot's. About this period, his brother-in-law, M. Drack, [1] having become a Catholic, Deutz, enraged at this conversion, uttered such fearful threats that Drack applied to the police for protection. Nevertheless, two or three years afterwards, Deutz's judaical fanaticism had subsided so considerably, that he even declared his intention of himself embracing the Catholic faith, and for this purpose solicited, through his brother-in-law, an audience of the Archbishop of Paris.

During the progress of his conversion, this prelate, thinking that it would probably be more rapid and more efficacious at Rome,

---

1. M. Drack was a Jewish Rabbi, and his conversion made a great noise at Paris some years ago. Tr.

advised him to proceed thither. Deutz accordingly performed this journey in the beginning of the year 1828. M. de Quelen [2] recommended him in the strongest terms to Cardinal Capellari, then Prefect of the Propaganda, and now Gregory XIV. Leo XII. the then reigning pope, directed Archbishop Ostini to instruct him in the Catholic religion.

For some time, and on several occasions, Deutz seemed to waver in his resolution. In 1828 he wrote as follows:

> I have experienced some days of storm, and was even on the eve of returning to Paris without baptism. This was the last struggle of expiring Judaism. Thanks be to God, my eyes are now entirely opened, and in a short time I shall have the happiness of being a Christian.

He was at length judged worthy of baptism, and Baron Mortier, First Secretary of Embassy, was his godfather. An Italian princess was the other sponsor.

Thus it was by betraying his God that he exercised himself in the art of betraying man.

He was soon after presented to the Pope, who received him with the most benevolent kindness. A pension of twenty-five *piastres* [3] a month had been allowed him, the moment he arrived at Rome, from the funds of the Propaganda, His brother-in-law, Drack, being recommended to the Duchess of Berri by Baron Mortier, had been appointed librarian to her Royal Highness. It was at this period that, on the recommendation of the Pope, Deutz was admitted into the Convent of the Holy Apostles as a boarder, and he always continued to affect the greatest devotion in public.

Nevertheless, the persons who were intimate with him, easily perceived with what view he had made his abjuration. Most of his original patrons discovered that he was deceiving them, and abandoned him successively. He soon had nothing left but the support of Cardinal Capellari, who, seeing him but seldom, continued to feel the same interest in his welfare.

2. The Archbishop of Paris. Tr.
3. Five pounds sterling.

In 1830, Deutz, under pretence that he would no longer live upon charity, obtained from his patron, the present Pope, a few thousand *francs*, with which he left Rome, to settle, he said, as a bookseller, at New York. In 1831, he returned to France, after having spent the funds destined to purchase his stock in trade. From France he again went to Italy. At this period the Duchess of Berri, who was making preparations for her landing in France, was in search of a resolute and intelligent man to undertake certain missions of the highest importance, in Spain, Portugal, and Russia. The Pope mentioned Deutz to the duchess, as a man perfectly qualified for such an undertaking, and deserving of her fullest confidence. On this recommendation the Duchess of Berri decided upon seeing him.

At Massa, a town belonging to the Duchy of Modena, and situated upon the coast of Tuscany, he had several audiences of the duchess, but always in different houses. He set out, with instructions of the most delicate nature, which he fulfilled with great ability.

CHAPTER 12

Betrayal

Meanwhile time had sped on, and the Duchess of Berri, now certain of maintaining peace with the three great powers, should she succeed in placing her son upon the throne of France, had contrived to enter La Vendée in the manner I have described, and civil war had followed her thither.

Whilst this was passing, Deutz returned to Paris to assist, in conjunction with an agent of the King of Portugal, in raising a loan, which her Royal Highness and Don Miguel were to share equally, on condition that Don Miguel should furnish the duchess with an equivalent for part of the sum in arms and ammunition, which he was to land upon the coast of La Vendée.

It was at this period that, the attention of the police of Paris being directed towards these two men, one of them was recognized as an agent of the Duchess of Berri. Offers of a bribe to betray her were immediately made to him by subaltern agents of the Government; but Deutz chose to treat with the Minister of the Interior himself, who granted him an audience. This minister was M. de Montalivet.

What passed at this interview—what promises were made, and what offers accepted, remains a secret between M. de Montalivet and Deutz. But as the devil has always a hand in such treaties, they generally succeed. Nevertheless, though the instrument was found, there was great hesitation about using it. If the Duchess of Berri were arrested, she would come within the jurisdiction of the Court of Assize, which might very possibly condemn her to death. The king, it is true, enjoyed his prerogative of pardoning; but there are times when it is as difficult to exercise this power of clemency as that of inflicting death. On the other hand, leaving the Duchess of Berri to proceed in her plans was not without inconvenience. The Chamber of Deputies, however dull and easy, might in the end become as tired of civil war as of other things, and insist upon its being put an end to. In a word, M. de Montalivet remained in great embarrassment with his traitor, not knowing how to act, and quite in despair at having proved himself so clever.

About this period a ministerial remodelling took place: M. de Montalivet was appointed to the civil list, and M. Thiers took his place as Minister of the Interior. In this change, the youthful minister saw the means of getting rid of his Judas, by sending him to claim his thirty pieces of another. But Deutz raised difficulties. He had begun the affair, he said, with the Count de Montalivet, and would terminate it with him; he knew the Count, and was unacquainted with M. Thiers;—in short, after much talking, M. de Montalivet prevailed upon Deutz to get into his carriage with him, and they drove together to the residence of M. Thiers.

This gentleman was too penetrating not to have a suspicion of the discontent which his appointment had given, and too able not to attempt to gain popularity by striking an important blow. The capture of the Duchess of Berri would secure him the favour of the Chamber of Deputies, and the Chamber of Deputies he considered to be the whole nation, or nearly so. Hence M. Thiers might perchance become a national man.

Deutz accordingly set out for La Vendée, accompanied by M. Joly, a Commissary of Police, and arrived there under the name of Hyacinth.

A few days after his arrival, and doubtless for the purpose of concerting measures with him, M. Maurice Duval was appointed Prefect.

This unpopular appointment, the brutal dismissal of M. de Saint-Aignan, even the manner in which this gentleman received intimation that he was to be superseded, excited great discontent among the inhabitants of Nantes. Moreover, the reputation which M. Maurice Duval had acquired at Grenoble preceded his arrival at the city he was now appointed to administer, and told much to his disadvantage. Any single one of these reasons would have proved sufficient to have obtained for him an ordinary *charivari*,[1] but all these reasons combined led to his receiving one which, under the government of the majorities, might have been termed the king of *charivaris*.

On the 19th of October the inhabitants of Nantes were informed of the dismissal of M. de Saint-Aignan and the appointment of M. Maurice Duval, who was to have arrived the same day, but did not reach that city till the next. The most hostile feelings were immediately manifested towards him. Every individual among the populace, who possessed instruments of noise, such as stew-pans, metal porringers, cat-calls, and similar vehicles of "sweet sound," instinctively laid hold of them; they who had none, ran to borrow them from their friends; and lastly, those who had neither instruments nor friends resorted to the most whimsical means in order to play their part in the great popular concert about to be given.

Some ran through the city in search of all the little bells they could find, taking them even from the cows which chance brought in their way; others went to a foundry, seized upon a small bell just cast, which by means of a stick passed through the top, was carried on the shoulders of two men, and a walking belfry established. A general muster of knife-grinders' horns had also taken place, and more than six hundred individuals appeared with these instruments, which, as everyone knows, require no preparatory practice. A vender of whistles who, without this circumstance, would never have got rid of his dead stock, established a stall in the public square, and sold all his goods even to the very last article.

Between four and five o'clock, part of the musicians were as-

---

1. A hideous concert produced by the sound of kettles, frying-pans, and all sorts of noisy, jingling, and discordant instruments. In France, the *charivari* is used to express disapprobation or unpopularity.—Tr.

sembled, and they determined to do Monsieur le Prefet greater honour by going to meet him on his arrival. They accordingly formed themselves into *echelons* upon the road by which he was to reach the city. The authorities, having perceived this general enthusiasm, but fearing to stop it in its first *impetus*, dispatched a staff-officer to acquaint M. Maurice Duval with the noisy reception that awaited him. The new Prefect profited by this information, and, sending forward his empty carriage, entered the city *incognito*.

Thus for a moment did M. Maurice Duval outwit these inconvenient musicians. Nevertheless, the information soon spread that the new *prefect* had reached the Hotel de France, Place de la Comedie. The *charivari*-orchestra proceeded thither immediately, but the Place was too small to contain the whole of the performers. The body of musicians alone, like a great tarantula spider, fixed itself in the Place and spread its claws through the neighbouring streets.

Now a noise began, sufficient to rupture the brain of a deaf man. Persons worthy of credit, who live at a distance of two leagues from the city, have since affirmed, upon their honour, that they heard this dreadful noise at their houses. Nor is this surprising; for there were probably ten thousand musicians performing together; being five thousand more than Nero had, and everybody is acquainted with that emperor's taste for melody. During the loudest part of the concert, a man on foot made incredible efforts to get through the crowd and reach the Hotel de France, the doors of which were shut.

He was, however, forced to mingle with the *charivari*-musicians, and join in their chorus. This individual was no other than M. Maurice Duval. Next day, the new *prefect* took up his abode at the prefecture. The news of his installation in office convinced the musicians that their performance would not be thrown away, so far as regarded the individual for whom it was intended. Consequently, about four o'clock in the afternoon, the orchestra again assembled in the Place de la Prefecture. Here, it was still more numerous and more noisy than the night before.

It is, however, in the character of the French, soon to get tired of everything, even of a *charivari*, and on the third day, a considerable number of the musicians were absent. The authorities then thought they might with safety put an end to the daily serenade. Accordingly, between seven and eight o'clock in the evening, platoons of *gendarmes* and infantry of the line debouched in the Place, and occupied all the streets leading into it.

The musicians now thought, and with good reason too, that it was high time to terminate their performance; they therefore retreated from the troops, going on nevertheless with their *charivari* as they fell back, so that this retreat was attended with all the honours of victory.

Next day the city was perfectly peaceable, and M. Duval was enabled to publish a proclamation, in which he complained of being judged by his former reputation. Among other things, he said that his works should soon bear testimony of his patriotism.

Now, as the work upon which he most depended to effect a change of opinion in his favour was the capture of the Duchess of Berri, he began by taking measures to prevent the possibility of her escaping him. This naturally brings us back to Deutz.

We have already stated how jealously the duchess was watched by those around her, and that a *coterie* which had possession of her person prevented almost all her friends from seeing her. That circumstance had nearly rendered Deutz's treachery of no avail. This individual well knew that the duchess was at Nantes, but so far as that went the whole town was as much in the secret as he was. The house she inhabited was the important thing to know, and of this Deutz was ignorant.

He succeeded, however, in making her acquainted with his arrival; but the duchess, fearing at first that this information was a snare laid by the police, or that another person might obtain access to her by assuming the name of Deutz, refused to see him unless he entrusted his dispatches to a person whom she sent to him. This he declined doing, but stated that he was going to spend some days at Paimbœuf, and on his return he would, in the hope of being more fortunate, have the honour again to solicit an audience of her Royal Highness.

And in fact, he quitted Nantes with his companion, M. Joly,

who stuck to his person like a guard of the high constable's court. Both proceeded to Paimboeuf, the one stating that he had come to purchase an estate in the neighbourhood, the other that he was a land-surveyor, employed by his companion. They were absent ten days.

Deutz, on his return to Nantes, renewed his request to be admitted to the honour of an audience, but without any better success. He then consented to entrust a third person with the important despatches of which he was the bearer. On receiving these letters the duchess no longer felt any doubts about the identity of Deutz, and consented to see him.

Accordingly, on Wednesday the 31st of October, at seven o'clock in the evening, Deutz was taken to the house of the Demoiselles Deguigny. He had never been there before, nor did he then know where he was, or even the street he was in.

After a conference of an hour and a half, he took leave of the duchess, thinking at the time that she quitted the house when he did, and had received him as she had done at Massa, at the residence of a person devoted to her, and not at her own. He was unable, therefore, either to give any very precise information concerning the house in which he had seen her, or to affirm positively where she was to be found. It would, of course, have been folly to risk an attempt to arrest her, which might have produced no other result than that of putting her upon her guard.

Deutz therefore solicited a second audience, under pretence that the agitation caused by the sight of Her Royal Highness at the last audience she granted him had made him forget to communicate to her matters of the most urgent importance. The duchess felt less difficulty in granting his request, because she had herself despatches to give him. A second interview was therefore fixed for Tuesday the 6th of November, of which circumstance Deutz immediately informed the police.

At four o'clock, Deutz was conducted to the duchess; but it seems that he was followed by some skilful police-agents, who watched all his motions.

The same day, at about two o'clock, this wretch had passed

before the house in which he had first seen her, and was again to see her that afternoon, the better, no doubt, to reconnoitre the premises. No sooner therefore, had he entered the house a second time, than he made such observations as led him to suppose that the duchess resided there.

On reaching her apartment, he found her pale and agitated. She rose, walked straight to him, crumpling a letter in her hand, and fixing her eyes upon him as if she would scrutinize his innermost thoughts.

"Sir," she said, "do you know what they write to me from Paris? they inform me, that I am betrayed;—is it by you?"

Deutz remained silent at this unexpected appeal; he had not a word at command wherewith to defend himself.

"You see, Sir," continued the duchess, showing him the dispatch, "that I am to be arrested tomorrow. Do you know anything about it?"

Deutz, having recovered himself, assumed a certain degree of assurance. He attributed to wounded feelings the confusion he had betrayed on her accusing him, protested that he was innocent and faithful, and appealed for a proof of his incorruptibility to the economy with which he had executed every mission she had entrusted him with. The duchess acknowledged the truth of his appeal, and immediately said that she believed him incapable of such baseness. This audience lasted about an hour.

As Deutz withdrew, he passed near the door of the dining-room, which was ajar. Casting a rapid glance into the room, he perceived a table set out for seven persons; and as he knew that the Demoiselles Deguigny lived alone, he had no doubt that the duchess was about to sit down to dinner. On that day she had invited Madame de Charrette,[2] and Mademoiselle Kersabiec to dine with her.

Deutz immediately went to M. Maurice Duval, gave an account of what he had seen, and advised him to make haste so as to arrive before the dinner was over; for he was not yet quite satisfied that the duchess resided in that house. The *prefect*, that very

2. Madame de Charrette is a natural daughter of the late Duke of Berri.

morning, had concerted measures with the military authorities, who now that the city had been placed in a state of siege, exercised the supreme power. He therefore proceeded, without losing an instant, to the house of Count d'Erlon, after having first locked Deutz into a room, under the charge of a policeman, with orders not to quit him. This was done to make sure of his assistance and guidance. General d'Erlon having immediately sent to me, in ten minutes all my military preparations were made in concert with him, and the necessary orders given to Colonel Simon Lorrière, commandant of the city.

A large force was necessary on this occasion, for two reasons: first, because there might be a revolt among the population; and secondly, because it was necessary to surround a large mass of houses. Consequently about twelve hundred men were called out; they had received, early that morning, orders to hold themselves in readiness.

The two battalions which these men formed, were divided into three columns, of which I took the command, accompanied by Count d'Erlon, and by the Prefect, who directed the operation. The first column, commanded by Colonel Simon Lorrière, went down the Cours, leaving sentries along the walls of the gardens belonging to the bishop's palace and the adjoining houses; then proceeding along the moat of the castle, came in front of the Demoiselles Deguigny's house and there deployed.

The second and third columns, at the head of which I had put myself, crossed the Place St. Pierre, and there separated. One, which remained with me, went down the Grande Rue, formed a *coude* at the Rue des Ursulines, and joined, by the Rue Basse-du-Chateau, the column commanded by Colonel Simon Lorrière.

The third, after I had left it under the command of Colonel Lafeuille of the 56th went straight down the Rue Haute-du-Chateau, and joined the other two in front of the house of the Demoiselles Deguigny, which was thus completely invested.

CHAPTER 13

Hiding Place Discovered

Darkness had now begun to spread her mantle over the city, and the night was beautiful. The Duchess of Berri, from the windows of her apartment, saw the moon rise above the horizon upon a calm, dark blue sky. The massive towers of the old castle, silent and motionless, displayed their forms like a brown shadow upon the heavens. There are moments when Nature seems to us so mild, and so friendly, that, amid the calmness she displays, we cannot suspect that danger is lurking nigh. The fears excited in the Duchess of Berri by the letter she had received from Paris were wholly dissipated at this beautiful sight, when, on a sudden, M. Guibourg, who had approached the window, saw the glitter of bayonets, and a column of troops in full march towards the house. It was the one commanded by Colonel Simon Lorrière. He immediately started back, and exclaimed,

"Hide yourself, Madam! for God's sake, hide yourself!"

On reaching the *mansarde*, the recess was immediately opened, and a dispute arose as to who should enter it first This was really not a vain quarrel of etiquette and precedence: the passage into the place of concealment was by no means easy, and the soldiers might reach the *mansarde* before the last of the party could have time to enter it. The opening would then be closed, and this person, whoever it might be, taken prisoner. Moreover, the recess was so small, that two men would have found great difficulty in entering it after the females of the party had preceded them. The Duchess of Berri, however, put an end to the discussion by commanding that all should enter according to their stature, the tallest first. Thus M.

de Ménars was to take the lead, and M. Guibourg follow. But the latter gentleman reversed the order by entering first. The duchess and Mademoiselle Stylite Kersabiec still remained, and the latter at first refused to pass in before the royal fugitive. But the duchess with a smile said to her,

"In good strategy, Stylite, when a general effects a retreat, he always goes last."

Mademoiselle Stylite, therefore, went into the recess, the duchess followed her, and was in the act of closing the aperture when the soldiers opened the door of the room.

The troops had entered the ground-floor, preceded by M. Joly, the Commissary of Police from Paris, and likewise by the Commissary of Police of Nantes. Both these functionaries had pistols in their hands; and the weapon of one of them went off, from his inexperience in the use of it, wounding him in the hand. The soldiers soon spread through the house. It was my duty to invest it, and I had done so; it was the duty of the police-people to search it, and I allowed them to act without any interference on my part.

M. Joly perfectly recognized the interior of the building, from the description given him by Deutz. He found the dinner-table for seven persons still laid, for it had not yet been used; whilst the two Demoiselles Deguigny and Madame de Charrette seemed the only occupants of the house. He began by securing the persons of these ladies; then proceeding up the staircase like one to whom the locality was well known, he went straight to the door of the *mansarde*, and, having recognized it, he said in a tone sufficiently loud for the duchess to hear it from her recess:

"Here is the hall of audience."

There was now no further doubt in the mind of the Duchess of Berri that Deutz was the author of the treachery announced to her that day from Paris. An open letter lay upon the table; M. Joly took it up. It was the one which the duchess had that morning received from Paris, and which Deutz had seen her crumple in her hand.

The following is a note by General Dermoncourt:

The Duchess of Berri had agents at Paris among the individuals whom King Louis-Philippe considers the most devoted to him; and these persons gave her information of everything that passed in the offices of the Ministers, and at the Tuileries. It would, indeed, astonish the public, were I to name the party from whom she received the information alluded to; but my doing so would be a denunciation.

The general, who is the most amiable of men, can with difficulty make up his mind to give pain even to unworthy individuals. Being acquainted with every circumstance connected with the present work, I feel no hesitation in satisfying the curiosity of the English reader by filling up the *hiatus* left by the general. The writer of the letter informing the Duchess of Berri that she was betrayed and would be arrested if she did not immediately leave Nantes, was M. D'Argout, then Minister of Commerce, who had long made a practice of giving her secret information, and acquainting her with all the secrets of the cabinet of Louis-Philippe.

In the correspondence seized by General Dermoncourt, there were letters implicating several members of the French cabinet, more especially Marshal Soult the War Minister,—a brave and skilful soldier under Napoleon, a fawning hypocrite under the Restoration, and, it seems, a base and perjured traitor under Louis-Philippe. Of course these letters, after their seizure, were forwarded to the *proper authority,* which happened to be precisely one of the parties implicated.

Among the letters written to the Duchess of Berri, was one from Marshal Soult, stating that he would be "entirely hers" *(tout à elle)* on condition that she would re-establish, in his favour, the office of Constable of France. Her reply was very characteristic; it was as follows;

Monsieur le Marechal,
The sword of Constable of France is to be won only in the

---

1. The reader may depend upon the accuracy of these details—Tr.

field of battle; I await your presence there. [1]

This removed every doubt of the Duchess of Berri being in the house, and the sole object was now to discover the place of her concealment.

Sentries were immediately posted in all the rooms, and the troops closed every issue on the outside. The people had likewise assembled, and formed an enclosure beyond the soldiers. The whole population covered the streets and the squares; and yet no sign of royalism was manifested. A grave and solemn curiosity was evinced, but nothing beyond. Each individual felt the full importance of the event about to take place.

The search had begun in the interior: the drawers, and cupboards, and other pieces of furniture were unlocked when the keys were found, and broken open when they were not forthcoming. The sappers and masons in attendance, sounded the floors and walls, with hatchets and hammers. Architects examined every room, and having compared their external with their internal structure declared it impossible that any of them could contain a place of concealment. In one of the apartments, different articles were found, and among them printed papers, trinkets, and plate, which gave a certainty to the supposition that the Duchess of Berri was residing in the house.

The architects, on reaching the *mansarde*, declared, whether from ignorance or from generosity, I know not which, that there was less possibility of a place of concealment in those rooms than in any of the others. The police then proceeded to the adjoining houses, where they continued their search; and in a short time the duchess and her companions heard workmen hammering with all their might against the wall of the apartment contiguous to her recess. These blows were struck with such force that several pieces of plaster were detached from the wall, and fell upon the fugitives, who, for an instant, feared that the entire wall would fall and crush them to death.

Whilst all this was passing above-stairs, the Demoiselles Deguigny had shown great coolness and presence of mind. Though guarded by soldiers in the same room with them, they sat down to dinner inviting Madame de Charrette, and Mademoiselle Celeste de Kersabiec to follow their example. Two other females were also carefully watched by the police: one was Charlotte Moreau, the *femme-de-chambre* designated by Deutz as devoted heart and soul to the Duchess of Berri; the other was Marie Boissy, the cook.

The latter was taken to the castle, thence to the barracks of the *gendarmes*, where, as threats had no effect upon her, an attempt was made to bribe her. Sums, constantly increased in amount, were offered to her, and spread successively before her; but her unvarying reply was that she knew not where the Duchess of Berri was. As for the Baroness de Charrette, she passed herself off as one of the Misses Kersabiec, and, with her pretended sister, was conducted, after dinner, to the hotel of the latter, situated in the same street, about thirty yards higher up.

After a useless search, which lasted the greater part of the night, the police officers began to despair of success. They imagined that the duchess had escaped; and this idea was confirmed by their finding no traces of her in any of the neighbouring houses. The prefect, therefore, made the signal of retreat, taking the precaution, however, to leave a sufficient number of men to occupy every room in the suspected house.

He also directed the commissaries of police to remain there, and they accordingly took possession of the ground-floor. The circumvallation by the troops was likewise continued, and the national guard came and relieved some of the latter, who went to their quarters to get a little rest. From the manner in which the sentries were distributed throughout the house, it happened that two *gendarmes* were stationed in the very room containing the secret recess.

The poor prisoners were therefore obliged to remain very still; though their situation must have been dreadfully painful, in a small closet, only three feet and a half long, and eighteen inches wide at one extremity, but diminishing gradually to eight or ten inches at the other. The men, in particular, must have suffered great inconvenience, because in the recess, which became narrower as it increased in height, they had scarcely room to stand upright, even by placing their heads between the rafters. Moreover, the night was damp, and the cold humid air, penetrating through the slates of the roof, fell upon the party, and chilled them almost to death. But no one ventured to complain, as the duchess did not.

The cold was so piercing, that the *gendarmes* stationed in the room could bear it no longer. One of them, therefore, went down stairs, returned with some dried turf, and in ten minutes a beautiful fire was burning in the chimney, behind which the duchess and her friends were concealed.

This fire, which was lighted for the benefit of only two individuals, gave out its warmth to six; and, frozen as the prisoners then were, they considered this change of temperature a great blessing. But the good that this fire did them at first was soon converted into a most painful sensation. The chimney-plate and the wall being acted upon by the fire, threw out, in a short time, a frightful degree of heat which continued gradually to increase. The wall at length became so hot, that neither of them could bear to touch it, and the cast-iron plate was nearly red-hot.

Almost at the same time, and although the dawn had not yet appeared, the labours of the persons in search of the duchess, recommenced. Iron bars and beams were struck with redoubled force against the wall of the recess, and shook it fearfully. It seemed to the prisoners as if the workmen were pulling down the house and those adjoining. The duchess therefore expected, even if she escaped from the flames, to be crushed to death by the falling ruins.

Nevertheless, during these trying moments, neither her courage nor her gaiety forsook her; and several times, as she afterwards informed me, she could not help laughing at the conversation and guard-house wit of the two *gendarmes* on duty in the room. But their talk being at length all spent, one of them went to sleep, and slept soundly too, notwithstanding the horrible din close to his ears, proceeding from the neighbouring houses; for all the efforts of the searchers were now for the twentieth time concentrated round the recess. His companion, being sufficiently warm, had ceased to keep up the fire; the plate and the wall therefore gradually cooled. Meantime, M. de Ménars had succeeded in pushing aside some of the slates, so as to make two or three little openings, through which the fresh air from without renewed that in the recess.

Now, all the fears of the little party turned towards the workmen, who were sounding with heavy blows the very wall that protected them, and the plate of a chimney close to them, but belonging to another house. Each blow detached the plaster, which fell upon them in powder. The prisoners could perceive, through the cracks which this violence was every moment making in the wall, almost all the persons in search of them. They at length gave themselves up for lost, when, to their great relief, the workmen suddenly abandoned that part of the house which, from an instinct I cannot explain, they had so minutely explored. The poor fugitives now drew their breath freely, and the duchess thought herself safe; but this hope did not last long.

The *gendarme* who had kept watch, anxious to take advantage of the silence which had succeeded the noise made by the workmen, under whose efforts the whole house had tottered, now awoke his companion in order to have a nap in his turn. The other had become chilled during his sleep, and felt almost frozen when he awoke. No sooner were his eyes open than he thought of warming himself. He therefore relit the fire, and as the turf did not burn fast enough, he threw into it a great number of bundles of the *Quotidienne*,[2] which happened to be in the room. They soon caught, and the fire again blazed up in the chimney.

The paper produced a denser smoke and a greater heat than the fuel which had been used the first time. The prisoners were now in imminent danger of suffocation. The smoke passed through the cracks made by the hammering of the workmen against the wall, and the plate, which was not yet cold, soon became heated to a terrific degree. The air of the recess became every instant less fit for respiration: the persons it contained were obliged to place their mouths against the slates in order to exchange their burning

2. A celebrated Carlist Journal, published daily at Paris.—Tr.

breath for fresh air. The duchess was the greatest sufferer, for, having entered the last, she was close to the plate. Each of her companions offered several times to change places with her, but she always refused.

At length, to the danger of being suffocated was soon added another: that of being burned alive. The plate had become red-hot, and the lower part of the clothes of the four prisoners seemed likely to catch fire. The dress of the duchess had already caught twice, and she had extinguished it with her naked hands, at the expense of two burns, of which she long after bore the marks. Each moment ratified the air in the recess still more, whilst the external air did not enter in sufficient quantity to enable the poor sufferers to breathe freely.

Their lungs became dreadfully oppressed; and to remain ten minutes longer in such a furnace would be to endanger the life of Her Royal Highness. Each of her companions entreated her to go out: but she positively refused. Big tears of rage rolled from her eyes, and the burning air immediately dried them upon her cheeks. Her dress again caught fire, and again she extinguished it; but the movement she made in doing so, pushed back the spring which closed the door of the recess, and the plate of the chimney opened a little. Mademoiselle de Kersabiec immediately put forward her hand to close it, and burned herself dreadfully.

The motion of the plate having made the turf placed against it roll back, this excited the attention of the *gendarme*, who was trying to kill the time by reading some numbers of the *Quotidienne*, and who thought he had built his pyrotechnic edifice with greater solidity than it seemed to possess. The noise made by Mademoiselle de Kersabiec inspired him with a curious idea: fancying that there were rats in the wall of the chimney, and that the heat would force them to come out, he awoke his companion, and they placed themselves, sword in hand, one on each side of the chimney, ready to cut in twain the first rat that should appear.

They were in this ridiculous attitude, when the duchess, who must have possessed an extraordinary degree of courage to have supported so long as she had done the agony she endured, declared she could hold out no longer. At the same instant M. de Ménars, who had long before pressed her to give herself up, kicked open the plate. The *gendarmes* started back in astonishment, calling out, "Who's there?"

"I," replied the duchess. "I am the Duchess of Berri; do not hurt me."

The *gendarmes* immediately rushed to the fire-place, and kicked the blazing fuel out of the chimney. The duchess came forth the first, and as she passed was obliged to place her hands and feet upon the burning hearth; her companions followed. It was now half-past nine o'clock in the morning, and the party had been shut up in this recess for sixteen hours, without food.

The first words of the duchess were to ask for me. One of the *gendarmes* came to fetch me from the ground-floor, which I had chosen not to quit. Meanwhile, she delivered in charge to the other, a bag which incommoded her, containing thirteen thousand *francs* [2] in money, part of it in Spanish coin.

I immediately went upstairs to the duchess. My duty, as well as a sense of propriety, urged me to do so. Before I reached the garret, she had quitted the room in which the recess was, and I found her in the outer one in which she had seen Deutz, and which M. Joly had called the hall of audience. She advanced towards me with such precipitation, that she almost fell into my arms.

"General," she said, "I deliver myself up to you, and I trust myself to your integrity."

"*Madame*," I replied, "your Highness is under the safeguard of French honour."

I led her to a chair. Her face was pale, her head bare, her hair standing up over her forehead like that of a man. She wore a plain merino dress of a brown colour, burnt in several places at the bottom, and on her feet she had small list slippers.

As she sate down, she said, strongly pressing my arm, and in a short and strongly accentuated tone of voice: "General, I have nothing to reproach myself with; I have performed the duty of a

2. £500.

mother in trying to recover my son's inheritance."

The moment she was seated she looked round for the other prisoners, and, perceiving them all with the exception of M. Guibourg, requested that gentleman might be sent for. She then leaned towards me.

"General," said she, "I wish not to be separated from my companions in misfortune."

In the name of Count d'Erlon, who I was sure would do honour to my word, I promised they should remain with her.

The duchess appeared very thirsty, and, though pale, seemed animated like a person in a fever. I had a glass of water brought to her; she dipped her fingers into it, and its coolness seemed to refresh her a little. I then proposed that she should drink one, to which she acceded; but as the house had been turned topsy-turvy, it was no easy matter to get a second glass of water. At length one was brought, and she would have been obliged to drink it without sugar had I not thought of M. de Ménars, who was standing in a corner of the room.

It struck me that he was the kind of man likely to have sugar about him. I therefore asked him for some, as a thing I was sure he could give me; and in fact he took two lumps from his pocket. The duchess dissolved them in the water, by stirring them with a paper-cutter. As for a spoon, it was useless to think of such a thing; had the house been rummaged from top to bottom, not one would have been found. As soon as the duchess had drunk, she made me sit on a chair near her, for until then I had remained standing.

CHAPTER 14

Under Arrest

Meantime, my secretary had gone to Count d'Erlon, and my *aid-de-camp* to M. Maurice Duval, to acquaint them with what had occurred, and to request their immediate attendance. M. Duval arrived first.

He entered the room in which we were sitting, with his hat upon his head, as if there was not a female prisoner there who, from her rank and misfortunes, was deserving of greater deference and respect than she had ever enjoyed even during her prosperity. He approached the duchess, cavalierly placed his hand to his hat, scarcely raising it from his head, and exclaimed, "Ah! yes, it is she!" He then went out to give his orders.

"Who is that man?" enquired the duchess.

This question was certainly not out of place, because the prefect had appeared before her without wearing any of the badges which indicated his high office.

"Does *Madame* not guess?" I said.

She looked at me with a smile.

"It can be nothing but a prefect," she replied; and she could not have guessed nearer the mark had she even seen M. Duval's commission.

"Did that man serve under the Restoration?" she asked.

"No, *Madame*."

"I am very glad of it, for the Restoration's sake."

At this moment Count d'Erlon arrived, who observed on entering all those forms of politeness and etiquette which M. Duval had considered quite unnecessary.

"You have promised not to quit me," said she, addressing me in a whisper, and strongly squeezing my hand. I repeated my promise to her.

The duchess then briskly rose from her chair, and went straight to Count d'Erlon.

"Monsieur le Comte," said she, "I have trusted myself to General Dermoncourt, and I hope you will do me the favour to allow him to remain with me. I have asked him to permit that I may not he separated from my unhappy companions, and he has promised me this in your name: will you do honour to his word?"

"The General has promised nothing," the count replied, "which I am not ready to ratify; and in whatever you may ask me that is within my power to grant, you will always find me most eager to comply with your desires."

These words tranquillized the duchess, who seeing Count d'Erlon take me to a corner, went and talked to M. de Ménars and Mademoiselle de Kersabiec.

Count d'Erlon then informed me that the permission to remain with the Duchess of Berri extended only to M. de Ménars and Mademoiselle de Kersabiec. As for M. Guibourg, he thought it necessary that gentleman should return to the place in which he had been confined before his escape; he was the more strongly of this opinion because the judicial authorities would lay claim to his person, there being a criminal prosecution pending against him. The count also thought it expedient that the duchess should be removed to the castle as soon as possible, in order to avoid either a rising of the Carlists, or a riot among the people; for the news of her capture was already public, and the streets were crowded.

M. Maurice Duval now returned, and asked the duchess for her papers. She told him to look into the recess in the next room, and he would there find a white portfolio. The prefect went for this portfolio, and brought it to Her Royal Highness.

"*Monsieur le Préfect,*" said she with dignity, " the matters contained in this portfolio are but of small importance; but it is my particular wish to deliver them to you myself, in order that I may explain to you what they are intended for."

On saying this, she opened the portfolio.

"Here," she said, "is my correspondence; you will give it to the police; and here," she added, taking out a small image, "is a St. Clement, towards whom I feel a most particular devotion, more necessary to me at present, than ever."

I now approached her, and said that if she felt a little better, it was urgent we should leave the house.

"To proceed whither?" she asked, fixing her eyes steadfastly upon me; "whither would you take me?"

"To the castle, *Madame*."

"Ah! well, and from thence to Blaye, no doubt?"

Mademoiselle de Kersabiec then advanced towards me, and said: "But, General, Her Royal Highness cannot go on foot."

"Oh, *Madame*!" I exclaimed, "do not, I beseech you, lose time. The castle is only a few steps from this place. Throw a cloak over your shoulders; that is all you require."

"Come then," said the duchess; "as he answers for my safety, I must in some degree comply with his wishes. Let us go, then, my friends."

So saying, she took my arm, and we led the way.

"Oh! General," she said, casting a last parting glance at the *mansarde*, and the now open chimney-plate, "if you had not waged war with me after the fashion of St. Laurence's martyrdom, which," added she, laughing, "was unworthy of a brave and loyal knight, you would not now have my arm under yours."

On leaving the house, the *prefect* opened the march with Mademoiselle de Kersabiec, the duchess and I following immediately after.

When we got into the street, the *prefect* requested the colonel of the national guard to take the other arm of the duchess, who conformed to this arrangement with a tolerably good grace. The troops formed a double line from the house of the Demoiselles Deguigny to the castle, leaving a space between their ranks, through which we walked. Behind the soldiers, the inhabitants were pressing forward, getting upon each other's shoulders, and using the most strenuous exertions to obtain a sight of the captives. They formed a line, so far as the ground would allow, ten times thicker than that of the soldiers. Among these men who looked at us, were to be seen eyes flashing fire, and many other symptoms of bitter hatred. Low murmurs, but of deadly import, greeted us on our passage, and some shouts began to vibrate through the air. I stopped and looked round on both sides alternately; and I commanded by expressive signs the respect due to a woman, more especially when that woman was a prisoner.

Fortunately, the distance to the castle was very short, being not more than sixty yards. I must add, that even this distance would have been too great for the duchess, but for the respect and deference with which we surrounded her. Our own bearing towards her enforced the silence of the multitude, who had been reduced to great privations and suffering from the civil war which for the last six months had raged round the city of Nantes, destroying its trade and decimating its children. We at length reached the castle, crossed the drawbridge, and the gate closed upon us. Now only did I begin to breathe freely; as for the duchess, she had during our walk evinced no other mark of fear than that of pressing my arm strongly.

She then began to ascend the stairs, but had become so weak from the various kinds of emotion she had lately undergone, that I was obliged to apply my whole strength to support her. On reaching the apartment of the colonel of artillery, who was governor of the castle, and who immediately gave it up for her use, she felt a little revived, and told me she would willingly take something to eat.

"For," she added, "I was just going to dinner when you came, and I have eaten nothing for the last thirty-six hours."

Breakfast was therefore immediately prepared for the duchess. She ate with a tolerably good appetite, and this seemed to revive her, although she expected, she said, an attack of tertian fever, which came regularly every third day.

The duchess expressed a desire to write to her brother the King of Naples, and to her sister the Queen of Spain.

"I have only," she said, "to make known to them my unhappy adventure. I greatly fear they will be uneasy about my health, and that, from the distance we are removed from each other, false reports have been made to them."

"*Apropos!*" she added; "what think you of my sister's conduct in Spain?"

"I think, *Madame*," I replied, "that she is pursuing a right course."

"So much the better," said the duchess sighing, " provided she reaches a good consummation. Louis XVIII. began as she has done."

I now asked permission of the duchess to take my leave of her, as Count d'Erlon and the *prefect* were reviewing the troops, and I was under the necessity of being present

"When shall I see you again?" she said.

"Whenever your Royal Highness chooses to send for me. You know, *Madame*, that I am entirely at your orders."

"And would you attend to them?" said she smiling.

"I should consider it both an honour and a duty to do so," I replied. I then bowed and left the room

Scarcely had I advanced thirty paces from the castle, when a trumpeter of *gendarmerie* overtook me, out of breath, and told me that the Duchess of Berri commanded me to return to her that minute; he added, that Her Royal Highness seemed in a great rage with me. I asked him if he knew the cause of this sudden anger. He replied that, from some words which the duchess had said to Mademoiselle de Kersabiec, he attributed it to the circumstance of M. de Ménars having been taken to the tower instead of to an apartment next to hers. Fearing that all the respect and attention which I had directed to be shown to this gentleman might not have been paid him, I immediately went to his apartment, and found him so ill, that he had thrown himself upon his bed without having strength to undress himself. I offered to act as his *valet-de-chambre*, but as there was yet neither chair nor table in his room, and he could not stand, this was by no means an easy office. I therefore called a *gendarme* to my assistance, and we succeeded in putting him into bed. When this was done, I informed him that the duchess had just sent a messenger for me, and that we should probably have some altercation in consequence of his being separated from her. He requested me to tranquillize her with respect to his illness, and to tell her that he felt it to be only a momentary weakness. To avert as much as possible the storm I was to encounter, he advised me to dwell a great deal upon his being very much pleased with his apartment.

I immediately proceeded to the apartment of the duchess. The moment she saw me she hounded rather than walked towards me.

"Ah, ah! Sir," she said, in a voice of great anger; "ah! it is thus you begin; it is thus you keep your promises; this is of good augury for the future; this is dreadful."

"What is the matter, *Madame?*" I asked.

"The matter is, that you promised not to separate me from any of my companions, and you have already begun by placing Ménars in another building."

"*Madame*, you are mistaken," I said; "M. de Ménars is in the tower, it is true; but the tower belongs to the *corps-de-logis* inhabited by your Royal Highness."

"True; but to get at it, we must descend our own staircase, and ascend another."

"Your Royal Highness is again mistaken," I returned. "You may proceed to the apartment of M. de Ménars by descending to the first floor, and following the line of apartments."

"If this be the case, come with me then, Sir; I will go and see poor Ménars this instant."

So saying, she took my arm, and attempted to drag me towards the door. I stopped her—

"Does your Royal Highness forget," I said, "that you are under arrest?"

"Ah! that is true," said she, sighing; "I thought myself still in a palace, but I am in a prison. At all events, General, I hope I am not forbidden to send and inquire how he is?"

"I am come to tell your Royal Highness how he is, for I have just left him."

"Well! how is he?"

I then acquainted her with what I had done. These marks of attention, which she considered an act of kindness to herself much more than to M. de Ménars, affected her a good deal.

"General," she said, in a tone which showed that her anger had entirely subsided, "I thank you for your kindness to Ménars. He is well worthy of it, for he was no advocate for my silly enterprise. He urged everything he could to dissuade me from it; but when he saw that I was fully bent upon it, he said to me, 'Madame, I have now been with you sixteen years, and it is my duty to follow you: but in so doing, it is without approving of your projects, which may produce the most unhappy results both for yourself and France.'"

The duchess stopped for an instant, and then added with a sigh, "Poor Ménars was perhaps right."

Being now too late for the review, I remained with the duchess until the dinner-hour. On dinner being announced, I offered my arm to conduct her to the dining-room.

"If I did not think, General," she said, "that people would accuse me of attempting to seduce you from your allegiance, I would ask you to partake of my meal."

"And I, Madame," was my answer, "did I not fear being seduced, would willingly accept your invitation; for I have taken nothing since yesterday morning at eleven o'clock."

"What!" she exclaimed, "did you not dine yesterday?"

"No more than your Royal Highness did."

"Then I should be wrong to be angry with you:" she said, "we are now quits. Apropos," she continued, "if I am in prison, I hope I am not to be prevented from seeing my friends, and that M. Guibourg may be allowed to dine with me?"

"I see no objection to it," I replied, "and the less so, because it is probably the last time he will have that honour."

Whether she did not hear these words, or whether she paid no attention to them, I do not know, but she made no reply; and as we had reached the dining-room, she seated herself at the table. I remained standing near her.

"*Apropos*, General," she said, "may I be allowed to receive the public journals?"

"I have no objection, *Madame*," I replied, "provided your Royal Highness will state those you wish to read."

"Let me see. In the first place the *Echo,* the *Constitutionnel,* and the *Quotidienne"*

"The *Constitutionnel, Madame*! do you read that?"

"Why not?"

"Are you ready to abjure your politics as Henry IV. did his religion, and say, 'Paris is well worth a charter?'"

"Think you that the contents of that paper could convert me?"

"The paper is certainly very powerful in argument, and capable of leading to profound conviction."

"No matter; I will run the risk. I should like also the *Courrier Français.*"

"The *Courrier!* really your Royal Highness does not reflect; you will become a Jacobin."

"Hear me, General:—the fact is, I all that is frank and honourable, and the *Courrier* is frank and honourable, I wish to have, besides, *L'Ami de la Chartee."*

"Oh! really —"

"This last, General, is from another motive," she said, in a tone of deep sadness. "In it I am always called Caroline; it is the name of my childhood, and I regret it, because that which has been conferred upon me in my womanhood has never brought me good fortune."

At this instant, M. Maurice Duval entered. He had just left the review, and, as on the former occasion, he dispensed with the ceremony of being announced, and he again merely touched his hat, which remained upon his head. It seems that, on that day, the *prefect* so far resembled the Duchess of Berri, that he was very hungry. He went straight to the sideboard, on which a dish of partridges just taken from the dinner-table had been placed.

Having called for a knife and fork, he began to eat with his back turned towards the duchess, who, having looked at him with an expression of countenance I shall never forget, turned her eyes towards me.

"General," she said, "do you know what I regret most in the rank I have lost?"

"No, *Madame.*"

"Two ushers to punish that man's insolence."

The *prefect's* conduct filled Her Royal Highness with such indignation, that she continually returned to the subject, and every now and then would squeeze my arm, and say:

"His hat upon his head!—his hat upon his head!"

CHAPTER 15

Ending

It was on the eventful occasion I have related in the two preceding chapters, that I saw the Duchess of Berri for the first time, and I confess that the impression she made upon me will never be effaced.

Marie Caroline, like all young Neapolitan girls, of whatever rank or station, has received scarcely any education. With her, all is nature and instinct. She is a creature of impulse; the exigencies of etiquette are insupportable to her, and she is ignorant of the very forms of the world. She allows her feelings to carry her away, without attempting to restrain them; and when any one has inspired her with confidence, she yields to it without restriction. She is capable of supporting the greatest fatigue, and encountering the most appalling danger, with the patience and courage of a soldier.

The least contradiction exasperates her—then her naturally pale cheeks become flushed; she screams, and jumps about, and threatens, and weeps by turns, like a spoiled child; and then again, like a child, the moment you give way to her, and appear to do what she desires, she smiles, is instantly appeased, and offers you her hand. Contrary to the general nature of princes, she feels gratitude, and is never ashamed to own it.

Moreover, hatred is foreign to her nature; no gall ever tinged her heart even against those who have done her the most injury. Whoever sees her for an hour becomes well acquainted with her character; whoever sees her for a whole day, becomes acquainted with all the qualities of her heart.

Next morning at ten o'clock, the colonel of artillery, commandant of the castle, called upon me, to announce a fresh burst of passion on the part of the duchess. Its cause was somewhat similar to that which had occurred on the preceding evening.

M. Guibourg, as Count d'Erlon had informed me would be the case, had been removed, during the night, to his former prison, so that, when the duchess inquired why he did not come to breakfast, and this circumstance was made known to her, for which my observation on the preceding day was intended to prepare her, she exclaimed against my treachery, and called me a *Jesuit*. This injurious appellation was so singularly ridiculous, as proceeding from the Duchess of Berri, that my laughter had not yet subsided when I reached the castle.

She received me with the same petulance as on the day before, and used nearly the same expressions.

"Ah! is that the way you act, Sir? I should never have thought it possible. You have basely betrayed me."

I feigned surprise, as I had done on the former occasion, and asked her what was the matter.

"The matter is, that Guibourg has been carried off during the night, and conveyed to prison, notwithstanding the promise you made me that I should not be separated from my companions in misfortune."

"General d'Erlon understood, *Madame*, by your words 'my companions in misfortune' only those who had shared in your fatigues and your perils: namely, Mademoiselle de Kersabiec and M. de Ménars. Accordingly, neither the one nor the other has been separated from you. You see, therefore, *Madame*, that neither General d'Erlon nor I have violated the word we gave to your Royal Highness."

"But why did you not give me notice of what was to take place?"

"I am not to blame on that point either, since, when I consented to M. Guibourg dining with your Royal Highness yesterday, I added that I felt the less objection to it, because it was probably the last time he would have that honour."

"I did not hear that."

"The General nevertheless said so, *Madame*," said Mademoiselle de Kersabiec mildly.

"But why not have explained the matter to me more clearly?"

"Because," I replied, "your Royal Highness had encountered so many shocks during the day, that I wished you to pass at least a good night; and I was certain that if you knew M. Guibourg was to be removed to prison during the night you would not sleep."

"And you, Stylite, why did you say nothing to me on the subject, since you understood the General's meaning?"

"From the same reason that influenced the General, *Madame*."

"Oh, if you are all against me, I shall have no chance. But I have had enough of war; and then for better or worse," she added, looking mildly at me, and holding out her hand, "why—but is he not a good creature, Stylite?"

"Yes, *Madame*; and it is very unfortunate he will not join our party."

I dropped the hand of the duchess which I held.

"All the respect that your Royal Highness is entitled to, you may claim from me; every service you may ask of me, which lies within the compass of my ability, I will cheerfully perform, and consider myself fortunate in being able to do so; your every wish also, if I can guess it, I will anticipate—" I suddenly stopped.

"But why say all this?" said the duchess.

"I will," I continued "ask your Royal Highness only one thing in return, which is to request Mademoiselle Stylite never to allude to the same subject again."

"You hear this, Stylite?" said the duchess. "Let us talk of something else. Did you ever see my son, General?"

"I never had that honour, *Madame*."

"Well, he is a brave child; very mad like me, very obstinate like me; but, like me, devoted body and soul to France."

"You love him much, no doubt?"

"As dearly as a mother can love her son."

"Such being the case, your Royal Highness must allow me to observe that I cannot comprehend how, after all was over in La Vendée, when, after the actions at Vieillevigne and La Penissière, all hope was lost, you did not think of returning to that son whom you love so dearly. We gave you plenty of time and opportunity."

"General, I think it was you who seized my correspondence?"

"It was, *Madame*"

"And you read my letters?"

"I committed that indiscretion."

"Well, you must have seen in them that, from the moment I had come to put myself at the head of my brave Vendeans, I resolved to submit to all the consequences of the insurrection. What! they rose for me, they risked their lives for me, and I could desert them! Never, General:—I promised that their fate should be mine, and I have kept my word with them. Besides, I should have been your prisoner long ago; I should have given myself up to you, to put an end to the thing, but for one fear."

"May I ask what that was?"

"I knew very well that as soon as it was known I was a prisoner, I should have been claimed by Spain, Prussia, and Russia. The French Government, on the other hand, would have had me tried, which is natural enough. The Holy Alliance would never have suffered me to appear before a Court of Assize; for the dignity of every crowned head in Europe would be compromised by it. From such a conflict of interest to coldness, and from coldness to war, is only a step; and I have already told you that I would never become a pretence for a war of invasion. 'Everything for France and through France' was the motto I had adopted, and from which I had determined not to depart. Besides, who would assure me that France, if once invaded, would not be divided. I will have the whole of it, or none!"

I smiled.

"What are you laughing at?" she said.

I bowed without making any reply.

"Come," she said, "tell me what you are laughing at. I insist upon knowing."

"I am laughing at seeing in your Royal Highness so great a dread of foreign war."

"And so little of civil war. That is what you mean, is it not?"

"I beg your Royal Highness to observe that you have completed my thought, but not my sentence."

"Oh! I don't feel at all annoyed or offended at this; for I came to France under an illusion with regard to the public feeling. I thought that the whole kingdom would rise in my favour, and that the army would join me. In short, I expected a species of return from Elba. After the actions at Vieillevigne and La Penissière, I gave positive orders to all my Vendeans to return to their homes; for I am a Frenchwoman above all things, General, and a proof of it is, that if I only turn towards those good French faces I see in this place, I fancy myself no longer in prison. The whole of my fear is that I shall be sent elsewhere. I am sure they will not leave me here; I am too near the focus of insurrection. No matter: they are more embarrassed than I am, General; you may depend upon that."

As she uttered these words, she rose and walked about the room like a man, with her hands behind her back. An instant after, she stopped short:

"*Apropos*, General! among the articles which you were so kind as to undertake to send me, and which I have received, there ought to have been a box of bonbons; but it was not among them."

I had the box in my pocket; I took it out and opened it. There were no bonbons; it was empty.

"Ah!" said the duchess, "it is empty. And in fact, it contained bonbons, and bonbons may be eaten."

"What kind of bonbons does your Royal Highness prefer? I will do myself the honour of sending some, for bonbons may also be offered as well as eaten."

"*Chocolate au rouleau,* with *dragees* upon it."

"Then your Royal Highness will allow me to—"

"General, bonbons—may also be accepted."

It was half-past six, and the duchess was going to dine. I therefore took leave of her.

"Goodbye till tomorrow, General," she said with the liveliness of a child, "and pray don't forget my bonbons."

I left her.

At nine o'clock General d'Erlon took the trouble to come to my house, to inform me that he was almost certain of the presence of General de Bourmont at La Chaslière.

"If this be the case, General," I replied, "I will take with me fifty horsemen, and in the morning General Bourmont shall be here."

At eleven o'clock I was on the road.

At twelve, the Duchess of Berri, Mademoiselle Stylite de Kersabiec, and M. de Ménars were roused from their slumbers, and forced into a carriage which took them to Fosse, where a steamboat was in readiness for them, on board of which were M. Polo, Adjunct of the *maire* of Nantes—M. Robineau de Bougon, Colonel of the National Guard—M. Rocher, Port-Ensign of the squadron of artillery belonging to the same guard—M. Chausserie, Colonel of *Gendarmerie*—M. Petit-Pierre, town Adjutant of Nantes—and M. Joly, Commissary of Police from Paris. The duchess was accompanied to the steamboat by General d'Erlon, M. Ferdinand Favre and M. Maurice Duval. On alighting from the carriage, the duchess looked about for me, and not seeing me, asked where I was. She was informed that I was gone on an expedition.

"Well, well," said she, "this is another of your acts of kindness."

The general commanding the division, the *prefect*, and the *maire* of Nantes were to accompany the duchess as far as Saint-Nazaire, and not to quit her until he had embarked on board the brig *Capricieuse*.

On entering the steamboat, the duchess asked whether M. Guibourg was to follow her. The *prefect* replied that such a thing was out of the question. She then asked for pen, ink, and paper, and wrote him the following note:

"I have claimed my old prisoner, and they are going to write about it. God will assist us, and we shall meet again. Kind greetings to all our friends! May God preserve them! let us have courage and confidence in Him! St. Ann is the *patroness* of all of us natives of Britanny."

This note was intrusted to M. Ferdinand Favre who punctually delivered it to M. Guibourg.

At four o'clock in the morning, the steamboat started, gliding silently through the sleeping city, and at eight, the party were on board the *Capricieuse*.

Contrary winds detained them two days in the roads; at length, on the 11th, at seven o'clock in the morning, the *Capricieuse* spread her sails to the breeze, and, being towed by the steamboat three leagues out to sea, sailed majestically on, and four hours after she had disappeared behind Point Pornic.

I returned to Nantes on the 9th, at five o'clock in the morning, having, as may well be imagined, found nobody at the *chateau* of La Chaslière.

I have not seen the Duchess of Berri since, and I have nothing more to say about her.

Let another now undertake the task of relating the third act of the drama, which began *à la* Marie-Therèse, and has ended *à la* Marie-Louise.

Following the failure of her rebellion in the Vendée, Caroline was arrested and imprisoned in November 1832. She was released in 1833 after revealing a secret marriage to an Italian nobleman Ettore Carlo Lucchesi-Palli—the Duke of Grazia—and delivered a baby daughter. She returned to live in Sicily, was ostracised by the Bourbons and died in 1870.

Appendix

No. 1

THIRD MILITARY DISTRICT.

TABLE of the Curé, Officiating Priests, and Vicaires of the Communes composing the Military District of Ascenin, with Observations relative to their Political Conduct.

Bailie Joue	CLORUITE BRUNS	33 42	Curé Officiating Priest	Sings the *Domine salvum fac regem Ludovicum Philippum.* Sings the *Domine salvum fac regem Ludovicum Philippum*; but his comfort is not very regular. A furious Carlist.
Tréné Frane Peaneré	BOTTE HANUSE THISSATEAU	40 38 41	Ditto Ditto Ditto	Ditto. Does not sing the *Domine salvum fac regem Philippum.* His conduct is by no means regular.
Varches	PIZAVEY	43	Curé	Does not sing the *Domine salvum fac regem Philippum*; but nothing improper has been remarked in his conduct.
Montabain St. Hertlion	PUOUZUB BAMEIAINS	46 53	Officiating Priest Ditto	Sings the *Domine salvum fac regem Philippum.* Does not sing the *Domine salvum fac regem Philippum.* His political conduct and proceedings require to be watched.
La Roucières Bellicon	MAZE MANOW	40 43	Curé Officiating Priest	Does not sing the *Domine salvum fac regem Philippum.* Does not sing the *Domine salvum fac regem Philippum*; but he does not meddle with politics.
Mannaesm	BEREUT	38	Ditto	Does not sing the *Domine salvum fac regem Philippum*, and is opposed to the present Government.
Pouttie Chapelle St Stein-par Saint-Mars	GEDARD	36 40	Ditto Ditto	Ditto. Does not sing the *Domine salvum fac regem Philippum*; but his conduct is good, and he does not speak ill of the Government.
Bannesure	GRELLURM	36	Curé	Sings the *Domine salvum fac regem Philippum.* On the 17th of June last, he asked *Ludovicum Philippum* not asked, a week after, that he should not sing it any more; want authority from the Bishop. He is a sound partisan of the Carlists.
	CRUAMOUTIE	32	Officiating Priest	Does not sing the *Domine salvum fac regem Philippum*, under pretence that he has no authority in the church from his Bishop; but he is designated with some of his brethren of the parish with politics.
St. Sulpice	TANUY	34	Ditto	Sings the *Domine salvum fac regem Philippum*, and does not meddle with politics.
Le Pin Ursa	GRELA HAMAIN	34 36	Ditto Ditto	Ditto. Does not sing the *Domine salvum fac regem Philippum.* It is a partisan of the Carlists, and commanded a Chouan in his house for fifteen days.

THIRD MILITARY DISTRICT.

TABLE of the Curés, Officiating Priests, and Vicaires of the Communes composing the Military District of Ancenis, with Observations relative to their Political Conduct.

COMMUNES.	NAMES.	AGE.	QUALITY.	OBSERVATIONS.
		Years.		
Ancenis	URIEN	64	Curé	Confined with the gout. *Tet heares to be badly disposed.*
	FRENEAU	37	Vicaire	Sings the *Domine* without adding *Ladovicum Philippum.* He omits [no political opinions].
	BROCHARD	44	Ditto	Ditto.
	DAVIAU	55	Ditto	Cannot now exercise his profession from ill health.
Mesanger	GOUY (Jean)	56	Officiating Priest	Sings the ancient *Domine* without adding *Ladovicum Philippum.* Manifests no opinion against the Government.
St. Géréon Anetz	ROUSSEAU	45	Ditto	Ditto.
	PITEAU	70	Ditto	Sings the ancient *Domine* without adding *Ladovicum Philippum.* In the presence of persons of importance, says nothing about the present Government.
Oudon	LEROUX	60	Curé	Ditto.
	ETIENNE	37	Vicaire	Ditto.
Le Cellier Couffé	JOSE	63	Officiating Priest	Ditto.
	PERRIGAUX	42	Vicaire	Ditto.
			Officiating Priest	Sings the ancient *Domine* without adding *Ladovicum Philippum.* Lately, he exhorted his parishioners, from the pulpit, to conform to the laws of the present Government.
Mouzeil	BRASCHAY	66	Ditto	A furious Carlist.
Ligné	BRIAND	44 {	Vicaire during the duty of the Curé, who is in prison	Sings the ancient *Domine* without adding *Ladovicum Philippum.* If, he manifested no opinion hostile to the present Government.

				Shags the *Domine salvum fac regem Ludovicum Philippum*. Shags the *Domine salvum fac regem Ludovicum Philippum*; but his conduct is not very regular. A furious Carlist.
Baillé Joul	CLOSTRE BRIDY	33 43	Curé Officiating Priest	Ditto.
Toffit Tiane Paunort	BOTTE HERNIN THIRAODEAU	46 38 41	Ditto Ditto Ditto	Does not sing the *Domine salvum fac regem Philippum*. His conduct is by no means regular.
Verdun	PRAULT	43	Curé	Does not sing the *Domine salvum fac regem Philippum*; but in doing his paper has been reclaimed in his conduct.
Montoinini St. Herlam	PROUST a HANNELIER	46 33	Officiating Priest Ditto	Sings the *Domine salvum fac regem Philippum*. His political conduct and proceedings require to be watched.
La Ronciere Billard	MARN MANOS	40 43	Curé Officiating Priest	Does not sing the *Domine salvum fac regem Philippum*; but he does not sing with politics.
Mammunsen	SECHT	38	Ditto	Does not sing the *Domine salvum fac regem Philippum*, and is opposed to the present Government.
Pouillé Chapelle St.	GORARD	36 40	Ditto Ditto	Does not sing the *Domine salvum fac regem Philippum*; but his conduct is good, and he does not speak ill of the Government.
Saint-Mars	GRELLIER	36	Curé	Sings the ancient *Domine*. On the 17th of June last, he asked employer; and sung it any more without ... after, that he should not sing it any more without ... from the Bishop. He is a strong partisan of the Carlists.
Benurere	CHARBONNIER	79	Officiating Priest	Does not sing the *Domine salvum fac regem Philippum*, under pretence that he has no authority in this effect from his bishop; but he is displeased with those of his brethren who meddle with politics.
St. Sulpice	TARSOT	38	Ditto	Sings the *Domine salvum fac regem Philippum*, and does not meddle with politics.
Le Fin Usse	GERLE HAMELIN	36 36	Ditto Ditto	Does not sing the *Domine salvum fac regem Philippum*. Is a partisan of the Carlists, and received a Chouân in his house for fifteen days.

No. 2

Instructions to the Commandant of the District of Clisson.

May 8th, 1832. Sir, I have just received your letter dated from Louroux, and I thank you for the particulars it contains. Although we may imagine that there is a great deal more of boasting among the peasants than of real intention to act, it would be advisable nevertheless not to neglect the information we receive, but to take our measures as if the thing was likely to happen. You must therefore redouble your vigilance, and press upon the commanders of your several detachments the necessity of keeping a good lookout both day and night, corresponding with each other, and mutually stating to each other the time of departure of their *patroles* from one village to another, fixing a point of union, so that one shall not march further than another. You will insinuate to them that they ought often to change the hours of starting these patrols, in order to prevent a too great regularity, which might be remarked by the Chouans, and enable the latter to elude our pursuit, as well as to make their excursions in safety.

You must also settle your plans in case of attack, and fix upon a central point of meeting for your battalion. It would likewise be advisable that, in each cantonment, the men were brought nearer together; for of your six hundred men, battalion complement, I find that only two hundred and thirty-five are in barracks, and it is a great inconvenience not to hare the men under your hand.

Louroux seems the place intended for these gentlemen; thither they go and make a parade of their bravadoes. It would therefore be advisable to observe that point with the most vigilant attention. Chapelle-Basse-Mer, Chapelle-Hulin, Vertou, St. Fiacre, and Vallet, being the cantonments nearest to Louroux, it would be very easy for the commanders of those posts to hold themselves in constant readiness either to proceed thither in any case of emergency, or each of them to send thither separate detachments. This is a plan that you should also lay down, so that they may be ready on the first alarm to act with promptitude.

You will commence this duty next Sunday, unless you receive counter-orders. You will make arrangements for the different detachments to calculate the distance they will have to march, so that that they may reach Louroux simultaneously, and as nearly as possible at the hour of mass; for it is probable that if ribands and other rallying signs are displayed, they will not be put on till after church; and as it has been declared by the Procureur du Roi that medals bearing the effigy of Henry V. and green ribands are seditious signs, and the wearers of them ought to be arrested, if any such are seen, your commanders of detachments shall immediately apprehend and send them, under proper escort, to Nantes. This measure shall always be pursued in future. Lastly, I request that you will make frequent rounds in the district under your command, to ascertain that your orders are punctually executed, and at the same time to obtain even the most minute intelligence, which under present circumstances may prove of great importance. I have the honour, &c.

No. 3

Report to Lieutenant-General Solignac.
May 13th.

I have the honour to report to you that the *chef-de-bataillon* of the 29th, commanding the military district of Clisson, and from whom I had received no communication for some days, has just written to inform me that his silence is owing to the excursions he has just personally made according to my instructions, and to those made in pursuance of his orders by his officers stationed near the places where the Carlists meet. He has gained no fresh intelligence, he says, and all appears quiet. The peasants have been silent for some days past, the nobles remain shut up in their *chateaux*, the legitimatist party are mute, and seem paralysed both physically and morally,—"of which," he adds, "we must not become dupes, as some indiscreet members of the party have been unable to refrain from stating that they were only waiting for orders, and must not stir."

The report of this officer coincides with what we see here, and in our own environs. It would seem that the party intend to pursue a more regular plan than that followed up to the present time; for it is notorious that they kidnap men and recruit their forces; that they are laying in stores of arms and ammunition; that their muster-rolls are complete in officers and non-commissioned officers; and that each commune has its men appointed, with orders to hold themselves ready to march on the first signal

The *chef-de-bataillon* in command at Machecoul has acquired the certainty that from a hundred and fifty to two hundred men belonging to that town receive regular pay; that some of the leading men of the place have been appointed chiefs of parishes and divisions; and that the funds applied to the payment of these men and to recruiting are deposited in the hands of a notary and of some confidential persons at Nantes. For my own part, I have received information that a considerable nucleus is forming in the environs of Ligné and Couffe; that the peasants, like those of Machecoul, are paid, and are trained in the barns to the use of arms.

Several workmen from Nantes, most of them belonging to the class termed pontoonmen, had proceeded to the place I have just mentioned; but they have almost all returned, and when asked the reason of their return, they pretend that it was because they were forced to learn the manual exercise. Their real motive is, however, that the rebels are waiting for orders. I am taking measures to be able to receive immediate information, should they again go out.

A certain K——, the eldest of three brothers, and who seems to hold a certain rank among them, resides at Couffe or in the neighbourhood. He stated, in a letter dated the day before yesterday, that they had already, in that neighbourhood, from twelve to fifteen hundred men enrolled; but for the moment they could assemble at most four hundred only, all of them, however, well equipped. This individual was to have come to Nantes last Friday; but he has written to say that important business, as well as orders he has just received, will prevent his coming for three or four days. I shall receive information of all these goings on.

From the above intelligence, it seems to me, General, that they are preparing for a bevy of bucklers, and I am also preparing to receive them warmly and make them repent their temerity. I have the honour, &c

No. 4

Circular to the Commanders of Military Districts.

May 22nd. The Lieutenant-General commanding the division, having informed me, what I knew before, that a very great number of Carlist emissaries are travelling through the departments of ancient La Vendée, for the purpose of exciting the inhabitants to insurrection, by spreading false intelligence and alarming reports, distributing incendiary writings and seditious signs, keeping malefactors in their pay, and carrying on a criminal correspondence with the factious in different parts of France; that these agents of disorder are going about with impunity under the disguise of beggars, pedlars, hunters, travellers, &c. &c; that they pass everywhere without the least obstacle, and enter even the cottages of the poor to enlist them in the rebel bands:—it is necessary to adopt measures for defeating the culpable projects of the enemies of the government; and it also behoves us to redouble our zeal and activity in supporting the civil and judicial authorities, and to exercise the greatest vigilance in order to detect the machinations of those promoters of riot and disorder.

I have therefore to request that you will give orders to all your commanders of cantonments, to search and examine with the greatest severity all strangers found travelling through the country; such as cannot give a satisfactory account of their presence at the place where they may be found, are to be forthwith sent before the nearest civil or judicial authority, which will adopt such measures regarding them as may be advisable.

You will appreciate, Sir, the full importance of these measures under existing circumstances; and, to leave no pretence for malevolence to calumniate our intentions, by asserting that we are acting illegally, you will direct your commanders of cantonments to use great discretion in executing these orders, applying them to individuals only whom they suspect of being vagabonds, or who may give reasons for supposing that, being strangers to the country, they are travelling through it with evil intentions.

I beg you will communicate this letter to the civil and judicial authorities of the military district under your command, in order to obtain their advice upon the best means to be used in the interest of the national cause, and for the good of the service. I have, &c.

No. 5

To Lieutenant-Colonel Paris of the 32nd, Commander-in-Chief of the Military Districts of . Ancenis and Chateaubriand.

May 28th. I have received your letter of the 22nd, dated Saint-Mars-La-Jaille, in which you inform me that, during several days, you have in vain pursued the bands supposed to be in the forests. They are perhaps very snug in the villages of the country in which they were seen; for we must now admit that a great portion of the population is formed into bands, and that, although they have remained inoffensive till now, notwithstanding their being armed, they are beginning to lift up their heads and assume a hostile attitude.

The *couvreurs,* or in other words the bands, are always the Same; and they find refuge among the inhabitants, because a considerable number of the latter are in the secret, and those among them who are patriots are too cowardly to dare to make the least revelation. Thus, my dear colonel, we shall have to encounter the armed population, and it seems they are only waiting for an opportunity to rise. Our enemies are everywhere, we see them daily without knowing them, and they will, they say, try their strength with us.

In this part of the country, we have been upon the alert for some days past, because they have had the address to spread a report that they intended to make an attack upon divers points; but it further appears that their plans want unity. Our being so scattered gives them great hopes. They would willingly force some of our smaller cantonments; but, being uncertain of success, and fearful that a check would prove of great disadvantage to their cause, they dare not yet attempt such a *coup-de-main.* No doubt, if their first efforts were successful, we should soon have a general rising.

It is therefore necessary to keep your attention directed towards the cantonments, and let the commanders of them be always ready to act on the first signal. Let them exercise the strictest vigilance, and those nearest together take measures for coming to each other's assistance. Let them have a point of centralisation so as to form a mass, and thus offer a more compact resistance; and, in the event of their encountering an overwhelming force, let them fall back upon the general point of union indicated by the chief in command. You will determine this point according to circumstances, in order to have all your forces under your hand.

I even presume that these arrangements have been already made, and that nothing now remains but to remind the commanders of cantonments of them.

You must, however, be aware, my dear colonel, that it would be wrong to persevere in the occupation of any particular cantonment, if such occupation were attended with danger. After having retired from it, you might again occupy it should circumstances change.

From what I have here stated, you must be sensible that the forces at your disposal must, at the same time that they put down the armed bands, serve to reinforce and support the cantonments in case of need. I have, &c.

No. 6

Circular to the Commandants of Military Districts.

May 28th, From the observations daily made to me by the lieutenant-general respecting the great facility possessed by the Chouans of escaping from the troops in pursuit of them, by taking refuge in *chateaux*, or country-houses, which they consider inviolable asylums on account of the difficulty, at a moment of crisis, of prevailing upon a judicial officer or a *maire* to legalize by his presence the entrance of soldiers into such houses, he has deemed it his duty to apply for orders to the war minister, from whom he has received the following instructions, which I lose no time in transmitting to you:

The minister states "that, according to the provisions of art. 48 of the *code d'instruction criminelle*, officers of *gendarmerie* are also officers of police assisting the *Procureur du Roi*, and may, in all cases where the parties are taken in the act of commission (same code, art. 49) perform every act within the competency of that magistrate. Among such acts are domiciliary visits in houses presumed to contain individuals proceeded against as having been detected *in flagrante delicto* (same code art. 14). Thus, the detachments sent in pursuit of malefactors or rebels may legally enter the houses in which such individuals may have sought refuge, whenever such entrance shall be legalized by the presence of an officer of *gendarmerie*, and on the condition that such officer forthwith reports his proceedings to the *Procureur du Roi*."

Thus you see, Sir, how advantageously this power may be employed in repressing the brigandage with which the country is infested, since your troops may penetrate into the sanctuaries of the rebels on being accompanied by an officer of *gendarmerie*; and you can direct your commanders of detachments to claim the presence of the nearest officer of that arm.

I have the honour, &c

No. 7

To the *Chef-De-Bataillon* Commanding the District of Machecoul.

May 31st. If, in pursuance of the instructions I have already given, you have not yet concentrated your troops, pray do so forthwith. The points to be occupied in your district are, Machecoul, Legé, and St. Philibert. It is upon these points that the brigades of *gendarmes* nearest to you are to fall back. I cannot urge you too strongly to impress upon your officers that, in these cantonments, they are to guard each other *militairement*. This disposition will last till further orders.

The communes left without troops must be patient. It behoves the patriots to show what they can do, and to procure resources in each locality. Let the national guard be assembled and send out *patroles*; its own security and that of the property of its members depend upon this. The period is rather critical, but it is in such moments that true patriots are known, and that the greatest exertions are to be made.

As we are on the eve of great events: hold yourself in readiness, and be upon your guard. Order your horrible forest of Machecoul to be explored at different hours, and on different days, and let me know the least thing that occurs. I have, &c.

No. 8

General,   June 1st.

It seems that our enemies, notwithstanding the check they have just received, as well by the failure of their attempt in the south, and in the several departments of the west, as by the important discovery of their plans in their voluminous correspondence, are not less disposed to try their fortune, and make use of all the means they have provided by attaching numerous partisans to their cause. You must have felt convinced of this on reading their correspondence, especially that of the duchess, dated La Vendée, May 18th. She expects that her friends will employ all their means to make her cause triumph.

I entreat you, general, to employ also all your means to defeat her plans. Do not lose an instant in urging the prefect to make an appeal to the national guard, and mobilize as many of them as possible. Let this be done at Nantes from this very day; there is much goodwill there, and a mobilization is already expected. Convert Vendean huntsmen into cavalry and infantry; let us turn our attention to the points of Ancenis, where we have artillery—Paimbœuf, where there is a depôt of gunpowder—and Machecoul.

These appear to be the points which the rebels will first attack, so far as I have been able to make out from the seized correspondence. I am assured that at this very time, there is a great assembly of rebels in the neighbourhood of St. Mars-la-Jaille, &c That country is very rotten. There is also another in the environs of Chapelle-sur-Erdre, and on the opposite bank of the river. This is M. de Laubépin's country, which may lead us to conjecture that Ancenis is to be the point of attack.

Our enemies are numerous, general; we must likewise endeavour to crush them by numbers. We have resources, and must make them available. Moreover, if these preparations were not necessary, they would nevertheless produce the best possible results, if they only alarmed our enemies and made them shrink back into their shells. Permit me to offer you reflections suggested by zeal and long experience.

I think the most important thing would have been to have marched yesterday in three columns upon La Vendée: the first from Maine-et-Loire, the second from Loire-*inférieure*, and the third should have been taken from the country itself, that is to say, from Bourbon-Vendée.

By means of a general *battue*, all the *chateaux* throughout the country would have been searched; alarm would have been raised in all parts of it, every project of meeting of the legitimatists would have been defeated, and perhaps a valuable capture might have been made.

The duchess must be somewhere in the country, constituting the centre of operations of her party. Who knows whether she would not have fallen into our hands; and so important a capture would have at once paralyzed the civil war. The duchess will get on horseback—do not doubt it, and we must be prepared for every event

I have given orders for all the troops to be centralized, and the isolated brigades of *gendarmes* to retreat upon the points occupied, which are near them. I have likewise ordered the district forces to concentrate upon Nantes, should circumstances render it necessary.

Another measure to be adopted would be to secure all those individuals at Nantes who went out to join the bands and returned; all of them are known;— further, to search every house inhabited by individuals notorious for their Carlism, and who have openly declared hostility to the present government. What have we to expect, if we stand upon ceremony with such persons?

I close my long letter, by intreating you to take my remarks into consideration, and as you know my intentions, I hope you will not take it amiss that I have offered you my opinion.

I have, &c.

No. 9

To the *Chief-de-Bataillon* of the 29th, Commanding the Military District of Clisson.

June 3rd, 1832.

As it may happen that today and tomorrow may prove stormy, I cannot urge you too strongly to be upon your guard, as a serious attack may be made. If the case were urgent, Vallet must fall back upon you, and Lourouz upon Nantes. As I give notice of this disposition to the commander at Vallet, it will be needless for you to send him orders on the subject.

You will retreat upon Nantes, if you are forced to do so. It is perfectly understood that this is not to take place till the last extremity. I doubt its ever coming to that; but as we must provide against everything, it costs nothing to determine upon our plans. You will recommend to your commanders of cantonments to burn cartridges, but likewise vigorously to use the bayonet, if those rascals appear: above all, no prisoners. You will send me tomorrow a summary list of the men present in each cantonment; also the condition of your cartridges, and the number each man has at his disposal.

I depend entirely upon you for taking every measure that circumstances require, and to which you may be forced to recur. I have, &c.

No. 10

To the Lieutenant-Colonel Commander-in-Chief of the Military Districts of Ancenis and Chateaubriand.

June 3rd.

From what the *chef-de-bataillon* Conty states to me, you were, immediately on your return, to have occupied the points indicated, *viz*. Derval, Chateaubriand, and St. J alien de Vouvantes. I find the first of these points rather too far distant from Chateaubriand, which is the pivot of your operations; but I believe its occupation to be important.

According to the instructions I gave you relative to the retreat which each commander of cantonment might effect, should he be forced back, Derval would fall back upon you, and so would

St. Julien de Vouvantes, and you under similar circumstances would fall bock upon Nantes.

I trust we shall not come to this extremity, but as it is not beyond possibility, it is seasonable to provide against such emergency. You will take care to send me immediately a summary table of the men composing each of your cantonments, the number of cartridges you possess, and the number placed at the disposal of each man.

You will join an account of the instructions you have given, according as circumstances and locality require. It is thoroughly understood that the cantonments are not to be abandoned until cartridges have been burnt, and that the moment the rebels appear they are to be fallen upon with the bayonet without caring for their numbers.

I hope you have made some use of your national guard, and mobilized the volunteers. I cannot too strongly recommend your directing all your commanders of cantonments to collect the whole of their men in one spot, from nightfall till daybreak, either in barns or other buildings. During the day, the men must always be ready to fall in, and must be prohibited from going far from their cantonments, as I have frequently observed that they do.

At the present juncture, my dear colonel, too much precaution cannot be used; for our enemies, though they have no idea of succeeding, intend, however, to make a last attempt.

I expect an answer from you by return of the orderly, with intelligence of all that may have occurred in your district.

No. 11

General,

In pursuance of the orders contained in your letter of this day, I have the honour to report to you the particulars of the occurrences in the battalion under my command, from the 3rd of June up to this day.

In the night of the 3rd to the 4th, about eleven o'clock, a band of Chouans appeared at Chapelle-Basse-Mer, whither Lieutenant George, who had received intimation of this meeting, sent a detachment of forty men under the command of Sub-Lieutenant Rudent. The rebels having run away on the first challenge, a few shots were fired at them. One Simoneau, an inhabitant of Chapelle-Basse-Mer was struck with a ball, and died on the spot. It has also been ascertained that another individual of the same burgh, named Bedureau was wounded.

Lieutenant George proceeded in person to Chapelle-Basse-Mer with the remainder of his forces, and reached this place at four in the morning; but all was then over.

On the 4th, at seven o'clock in the morning, I received notice that the tocsin had been sounded in the communes of Pallet, Monnières, Maisdon, and St. Luminé, and that the rebels were assembling at Maisdon. Having sent to ascertain the fact, I dispatched the company of grenadiers, the second centre company, and four *gendarmes*, under the command of Captain Giamarchi of the grenadiers, with orders to march up to the rebels and attack them warmly. This first column was closely followed by a second of about a hundred men, which arrived when the brigands were already in flight.

This affair being already known to you, I have thought that the above particulars would now be sufficient for your information. A serjeant of grenadiers was wounded on entering Maisdon.

The companies which had gone to St. Philibert by your orders, not having returned to Aigrefeuille till the 6th, at ten o'clock in the morning, at eleven I set off with my detachment, passing through Maisdon, where I had been informed there was powder concealed at the house of the *curé*. And in fact when I went thither, he delivered up to me, with a good grace, about thirty-five pounds of fine powder, together with some lint and bandages, the whole contained in two small bags which he had carried to a place a quarter of an hour's walk from his house, in order that he might not get himself into trouble, and which he declared had been left in his court-yard, but he knew not by whom. This powder has been sent to Nantes.

Same day, 6th, in the morning, M. Pinson, adjutant-major,

having been informed that the rebels were assembling at La Penissière de la Cour, a species of *chateau* belong to the commune of La Bernadière (Vendée), situated a league and half from Clisson, and intended to disarm the national guard at Cugan and La Bruffière, sent thither a detachment of forty-five infantry and two *gendarmes*. This detachment not being strong enough to surround the habitation, which stands in the middle of a vast garden, a *gendarme* was dispatched for reinforcements, and immediately other detachments, forming together ninety men, were sent to the assistance of the first, which, but for the arrival of M. Lesueur-Lenit, who had forty men with him, would have been forced to rail back—for armed peasants were arriving from all parts of the country, who stopped only on perceiving that they were too late to act.

On my arrival at Clisson, about half past three in the afternoon, I was informed of what was passing. I gave the men only the time necessary for taking off their knapsacks, and then marched them off in double-quick time to La Penissière de la Cour, where a brisk fire of musketry was going on. The troops were already in possession of the garden and the court-yard, and part of the house had been set on fire. Some of the Chouans, who had attempted to escape from the flames, were killed in the garden and the meadow contiguous; others succeeded in escaping.

According to the list of killed and burned made out next morning, about twenty were discovered who, from their dress and appearance, seemed to be persons of distinction. It is believed there was a priest among them, for a cassock was found in the house. The number of individuals in the house is not yet exactly known, but it is believed to have been about fifty. It is also thought that some are buried under the ruins, but this cannot yet be ascertained, for the fire is still burning.

On reaching the *chateau* I ordered the charge to be beat, when the soldiers in emulation of each other rushed into the house. At this moment three men were killed by some Chouans who had taken refuge in a dark place. This exasperated the soldiers, who, seeing the impossibility of taking these wretches prisoners, without running the greatest risks, could no longer be kept back, and in a moment the whole house was in a blase. The brigands were so determined, that during the action they kept shouting "Death to them!" "Henry V. forever!" and they played airs upon bugles, no doubt as a signal for assistance.

The conduct of every soldier present is deserving of the highest praise. Our brave fellows can only be accused of too great ardour, which is the reason why so many of them were put *hors-de-combat*. There were four killed and ten wounded, all belonging to my battalion.

I must not omit to inform you that in this action the *gendarmes* displayed great seal and courage; and that the national guard of Clisson equally distinguished itself.

On the 8th, a detachment of sixty men, twenty of whom belonged to the national guard, under the command of Captain Roch of the national guard, as localist, and seconded by Sub-Lieutenant Croisilles of my own regiment, proceeded to the village of La Hautière, in which they were informed that some Chouan chiefs had taken refuge, with the intention of forming a fresh band. Several individuals having fled on the approach of this force, some shots were fired at them, but without doing any execution. The village being surrounded, a Chouan was perceived by some grenadiers who ran to seize him. He fired, but luckily wounded no one, and in a moment he fell covered with bayonet wounds. It is presumed that his name was Bascher.[1]

This affair, without being of great importance, must nevertheless have prevented a meeting of the rebels, and struck terror into the whole country.

I had forgotten to state, General, that on the 5th, Captain Geoffroy, commanding officer at Vallet, being informed that there was a band of Chouans in the neighbourhood of Chapelle-Hulin, led a detachment thither. And, indeed, some armed individuals were seen running away as fast as their legs could carry them. A few men, sent forward as *tirailleurs*, tired about fifteen shots at them, killing two of the Chouans and wounding a third. The detachment, seeing the coast clear, returned to Vallet. Although this action was trifling, I have thought it my duty to report it to yon.

Though Lieutenant George, commanding officer at Louroux, took no share in the actions of the 4th and 6th, he did not remain idle. I have this day received a letter from him, in which he informs me that, by the imposing attitude he has assumed, he has succeeded in preventing the bands from increasing their strength in his neighbourhood, and that on the night of the 13th he arrested Messrs. de Landemont, and Landais-Cardinière, both of whom must now be in the prison of Nantes. The former, who was the promoter of the revolt at St. Julien, was taken with three pistols, a dagger, and some spare balls; the other had formed part of the band of La Vincendière, and was charged with directing the march.

I have already given you an account of the capture of six horses; but lest my report should not have reached you, I here repeat the particulars.

Being informed, on the 8th, that some persons unknown had gone to the farm of La Settière, in the commune of St. Crépin (Maine-et-Loire), with six horses, begging that they might be placed in the stable; that the farmer, fearful of committing himself, had refused to take charge of them; and that they had been turned into a meadow near that farm, the said unknown persons refusing to state to whom these horses belonged,—I sent thither a detachment under the command of an officer, who, finding the horses there according to the information received, brought them to me at Clisson. Among them I thought I recognised the horse ridden by M. Dudore when he was taken to Nantes.

On reporting this capture to Lieutenant-General Solignac, at the same time that I reported it to yourself, I received orders from the General to send the horses to Nantes, where, as I have been since informed, they were placed among those belonging to the *gendarmes*.

I enclose you the situation of my battalion, together with my report from the 11th to the 15th instant. I have the honour, &c.

George,
Chef-de-bataillon in the 29th Regt.

No. 12

Thirty-Second Regiment of Infantry of the Line.

Extract from an inventory made on the 4th of July 1832, by M. Bizeul, notary at Blain, serving to establish the state of the *chateau* of Carheil, and of all the furniture and moveable effects contained in the said *chateau* and its appurtenances. The inventory aforesaid being acknowledged exact, and signed by Captain Fatou of the 56th regiment of the line, was delivered to the several commanders of detachments of the 32nd regiment of the line, which successively occupied this *chateau*.

Thus, on the departure of the 32nd, the officer commanding it having demanded a certificate for the discharge of his responsibility, the Marchioness de Coislin delivered to him the following: "I the undersigned, proprietor of the *chateau* of Corheil, do hereby certify that the articles contained in the present inventory have been neither soiled nor damaged; that the whole property, gardens, fruit, and vegetables have been respected; that the troops behaved very well the whole time they were upon the estate, and I have no complaint to make against them from the said day on which the inventory was taken, up to the present time.

Carheil, October 31st, 1832.

(Signed) The Marchioness de Coislin."

A true copy of the above certificate. The members of the eventual Council of Administration.

Chapentier, Divivier,
Captain, acting Major.Colonel President.
Perriot. Jeanson.
Collette,
Military sub-intendant.

No. 13

Letter to the Marquis de Coislin,
In sympathetic ink.

General,

I have this instant received letters from La Vendée from a good source. It is but too true that the chiefs have been base enough to refuse *Madame* their assistance, and that to her very face. Her conduct is heroic: she says that, having implicated so many persons in her cause, she will share their fate, and not leave France. My young friend wishes to go and make known to her our good intentions. He would undertake this mission, general, if it met with your approbation. In the present state of things, I think you cannot do otherwise than send an officer of your *corps-d'armée* to Madame. Inviolable and respectful attachment.

No. 14

Draft of a Note which seems to have been addressed to the Marquis de Coislin, signed R. It is written in sympathetic ink.

Being unable to judge of the real state of public feeling, I have not, as may well be supposed, given orders which might not have been executed, but only notices, in order that our friends, being warned in time, might guard against the measures of our adversaries, and put themselves, for the public advantage, in the most powerful situation possible. The orders have been misunderstood; they were too minute and too lengthy. For the moment, we ought to confine ourselves to making known that *Madame* is on the French soil.

Signed R.

No. 15

Letter to the Marquis de Coislin.

M. Louis Renaud,

(This name was written in pencil.)

General,

I have this instant received the counter-order; I am sending everywhere in great diligence; I despatch expresses to the same places, and I write everything in duplicate. It is a great misfortune, and will cool the zeal of many; but I am bound to obey. Pray let me be kept acquainted with everything in the letters you write to me, and write in *cha* ink, on account of the process. Respectful attachment.

No. 16

Letter from Lerouz to the Marquis de Coislin,

In sympathetic ink.

General,

I have just received the report of the division which I have the honour to command, and I lose no time in despatching it to you. The counter-order has reached everybody, everywhere; only let us provide ourselves with everything. Proclamations have been sent to Nantes. I persist, general, in considering this counter-order a misfortune.

We should everywhere have taken the liberals by surprise, and our men, all of them ready, were filled with the greatest ardour, and now their ardour and their confidence are both diminished. I can do nothing unless I have three or four days notice. I had all my men under my hand; these brave fellows obeyed me like a regiment; now they are afraid of being deceived.

I will beg of you, general, at least to acquaint *Madame* and *Monsieur le Marechal*, with the preparations I had made. The officers who have agreed to serve under me particularly request I will state that they were ready to obey, and regret that the moment, to all appearance so favourable, has been let slip. Respectful attachment.

Signed, Leboux.

P. S. This ink is too greasy, and may be seen. I think lemon juice much preferable. If you wish for a better kind of ink, I can send you some.

No. 17

Letter from the Marquis de Coislin addressed to his son Adolphe, Tkrribn, Leboux, &c &c. informing them that the assumption of arms is fixed for the 3rd to the 4th of June. (See the order in the text.)

I send you, dear N———, a copy of the order which I have just received from *Madame*. You will there perceive that the assumption of arms is fixed for the 3rd to the 4th of June; that is to say, for Monday next.

You will therefore make your preparations, and issue your orders, so that the insurrection may take place everywhere at the same time. You will do, for the present, whatever you think for the best, and according to what you may agree upon.

Yours entirely, Renaud.

No. 18

Note (hand-writing unknown) addressed to the Marquis de Officers, containing the division of several communes on into six battalions.

1st Battalion.	2nd Battalion.	3rd Battalion.	4th Battalion.	5th Battalion.	6th Battalion.
Sect	St. Herblain	Bout	Sainte-Reine	Cambes	Plessé.
Grand-Champ	Bouron	Lavau	Pont-Chateau	Quilly	Le Gâvre.
Treillières	Couëron	Savenay	Drefféac	Gexarouët	Blain.
Chapelle-sur-Erdre	St. Étienne-de-Montluc	Chapelle-Launay	St. Gildas	Fégréac	Fay.
Orvault	Le Temple			St. Nicholas de Redon	
		Prinquiau	Sévérac		Bouvron.
St. Similien	Cordemais	Donges	Missilac	Avessac	
Chantenai	Malleville	Besné	Capelle-du-Marais	Gufmené.	Vignous.
La Basse-Indre.					

176

No. 19

Letter From Charrette To M. P.

Sir,   May 29th, 1832.

My travelling companion has directed me to inform you how grateful he feels for your kind offers of service. You may, therefore, place the sum you have mentioned, in the hands of his advocate Guibourg, who will give you a receipt for the same. He further directs me to assure you, that he has always depended upon your assistance to insure the success of his undertaking, the result of which, by no means doubtful I trust, will be known in the course of a few days. Hold yourself therefore in readiness, you and yours, to uphold interests so precious.

I am with distinguished consideration,

Sir, your obliged servant

Gaspard.

Letter From M. P. without a date.

Your note has just reached me. At eleven o'clock I start for our meeting, appointed to take place at La Croix-de-la-Mallière. At one, we are to be at the small down of La Barbotière; at three we are to take up a position in the neighbourhood of Bresson, and there wait for further orders. It is thought that on Tuesday we shall march upon Legé. Kind greetings to our friend who is at your house.

9 781846 776410